The Bridgestone food lover's guides to Ireland **The Traveller's Guide**

The Bridgestone
food lover's guides to Ireland:

The Traveller's Guide

JOHN McKENNA - SALLY McKENNA

ESTRAGON PRESS

First Published in Autumn 2001

by Estragon Press

Durrus

Co Cork

© Estragon Press

Text © John & Sally McKenna
The moral right of the authors has been asserted

ISBN 1 874076 39 1

Printed in Ireland by Colour Books Ltd

Written by John McKenna

Contributing Editors

Orla Broderick

Elizabeth Field

Caroline Workman

Publishing Editor: Sally McKenna

Editor: Judith Casey

Art Direction: Nick Cann

Illustrations: Aoife Wasser

Web: fluidedge.ie

For Connie McKenna

With thanks to

Colm Conyngham, Des Collins, Brian Condon, Frieda Forde,
Helen Kelleher, Sile Ginanne, Conor Cahill, Paul Willoughby,
Ian Vickery, Bernadette O'Shea, Paula Buckley, Judith Casey,
Maureen Daly, Colette Tobin, Catherine Tobin, Nick Cann, Pat Young,
Maurice Earls, Mike O'Toole, Ann Marie Tobin, Chris Carroll,
Paul Neilan, Ray Buckley, Gary Joyce, Kate and John Fraher

Bridgestone

...is the world's largest tyre and rubber manufacturer.

• Founded in Japan in 1931, it currently employs over 95,000 people in Europe, Asia and America and its products are sold in more than 150 countries. Its European plants are situated in France, Spain and Italy.

• Bridgestone manufacture tyres for a wide variety of vehicles from passenger cars and motorcycles, trucks and buses to giant earthmovers and aircraft.

• Many Japanese and European cars sold in Ireland have been fitted with Bridgestone tyres during manufacture and a host of exotic sports cars including Ferrari, Lamborghini, Porsche and Jaguar are fitted with Bridgestone performance tyres as original equipment.

• Bridgestone commercial vehicle tyres enjoy a worldwide reputation for superior cost per kilometre performance and its aircraft tyres are used by more than 100 airlines.

• In 1988 Bridgestone acquired the Firestone Tyre and Rubber Company combining the resources of both companies under one umbrella. This, coupled with an intensive research and development programme, has enabled Bridgestone to remain the world's most technologically advanced tyre company with testing centres in Japan, USA, Mexico and Italy.

• Bridgestone tyres are distributed in Ireland by Bridgestone/Firestone Ireland Limited, a subsidiary of the multinational Bridgestone Corporation. A wide range of tyres are stocked in its central warehouse and staff provide sales, technical and delivery services all over Ireland.

• Bridgestone tyres are available from tyre dealers throughout Ireland.

• Details of specialist Bridgestone and Firestone dealers can be found at www.firststop-eu.com.

FOR FURTHER INFORMATION:

BRIDGESTONE/FIRESTONE IRELAND LTD
Unit 4
Leopardstown Office Park,
Dublin 18
Tel: (01) 295 2844
Fax: (01) 295 2858

34 Hillsborough Road,
Lisburn
BT28 1AQ
Tel: 028 926 78331

website: www.bridgestone-eu.com

Introduction

Everyone is a food lover

The principle of this book is simple; it tells you the best food people and the best food places, and doesn't waste your time giving exhaustive lists and details of every possible choice. This is an independent book, and not some factotum trying to support Ireland's tourist industry. And so, these are the places we go to when we want to eat and when we travel with our family. This is the inside track on the best cooking and the best hospitality in Ireland.

No matter how simple the thing we seek, we always want to find interesting food cooked by interesting people, and served in interesting places.

The Bridgestone Food Lover's Guides tell you just who those interesting people are, describe the interesting foods they cook and the interesting places where you will find them. If you use this book you will eat well and find the most characterful places to stay throughout Ireland, whether you want a sandwich and a simple B&B, or a grand address to celebrate a special occasion in your life.

And, vitally, at its best, Irish cooking and Irish hospitality are not simply the equal of any in the world, but retain a uniqueness which makes them truly special. The pleasures which the people in this book offer and reveal to us, are the pleasures which make us all food lovers.

John and Sally McKenna
Durrus, Co Cork

Symbols

We have always been resistant to the idea that there is a hierarchy involved in assessing and judging places to stay and places to eat. We dislike the idea of Stars and Gongs, and the belief that at the top of the pile there is some place to eat or place to stay which is somehow 'the best'. For us, this is simply too reductivist, and denies many of the most interesting places in Ireland their true value.

cool

funky

So, rather than establishing a free-for-all amongst the places listed in this book, we have instead used the following symbols to illuminate the most pertinent character of the principal places featured. Please feel more than free to disagree with any or all of our designations! One man's funky, after all, can be another's man's bliss.

bliss

hot

formal

buzzy

chic

"PLEASE FEEL MORE THAN FREE
TO DISAGREE WITH ANY OR ALL
OF OUR DESIGNATIONS!
ONE MAN'S FUNKY, AFTER ALL,
CAN BE ANOTHER'S MAN'S BLISS."

How to use this book

● To use this book, you need a detailed map to navigate the country safely and surely, and a telephone or a computer in order to make reservations.

● We have given concise and precise details of every establishment, including e-mail numbers and web addresses whenever available. But please do note that prices and opening times are subject to change depending on the time of the year, and also telephone numbers are constantly subject to revision in Ireland, by virtue of added prefixes.

● With the conversion to the Euro in 2002, we have elected to give price ranges in the euro, ranging from € for inexpensive food and accommodation, to €€€, where prices are expensive for both food and accommodation. These can always only act as a guide, because a single à la carte dish in an expensive restaurant can work out cheaper – or, conversely, more expensive – than a full table d'hôte menu in a moderately priced restaurant.

● The book is arranged alphabetically by county, beginning with Carlow, followed by Cavan and so on. Some counties we have further subdivided into North, South, East and West, as is the case of Cork. Dublin is further broken down, into different experiences of food and accommodation, which we hope will make the book as accessible as possible.

● At the back of the book, there is a detailed index, listing towns, counties, names and addresses. Happy travelling!

Contents

NORTHERN IRELAND

INDEX

Carlow: where to eat

● Carlow food lovers have two key destinations. In the town itself, Sinéad Byrne has been dazzling the punters in **Lennon's Café Bar** with food that oozes God-bless-it deliciousness: roasted peppers with tomatoes and basil, topped with goat's cheese; fresh salmon salad with herb mayo; butterbean casserole with cider; beef casserole in Guinness served with colcannon. This is as smart as bar food gets. (121 Tullow St, Carlow, Tel: (0503) 31575. Open L, L€€)

● Another grand bar south of the town in Leighlinbridge, draws in what may be the biggest queues in the country on Sunday lunchtime. James and Mary Kehoe's **Lord Bagenal Inn** is an institution in Co Carlow, with cooking that is full of TLC, and particularly fab cakes and bakes made by Mary. Don't miss the wine list and the art collection, both of which show James Kehoe's wise discrimination. (Leighlinbridge, Tel: (0503) 21668. Open L&D, L€€, D€€€. Accommodation €€)

Where to stay:

Randall & Marie Dempsey's pretty and comfortable **Barrowville Townhouse** is just at the end of town, and is an ideal base. (Kilkenny Rd, Tel: (0503) 43324 Fax: 41953, barrowvillehouse.com, Rates €€) Bryan Leech and Martin Marley's utterly gorgeous **Kilgraney**

Country House is one of the ultimate cult addresses in Ireland. Superb, individualistic cooking and a loveable sang-froid from the owners makes this a dream getaway. Inquire also about their self catering accommodation. (Bagenalstown, Tel: (0503) 75283, Fax: 75595 kilgrany@indigo.ie, kilgraneyhouse.com, Rates €€)

Cavan: the inside track

County Cavan has one of the hottest pilgrimage sites for food lovers: Neven Maguire's cooking in the **MacNean Bistro** in Blacklion draws folk from all over the country for some of the most exciting food you can eat. Maguire is devoted to the art and craft of the stove, and his passion and skill in cookery is mesmerising. Don't miss the crispy Thornhill duck with 5-spice (the ducks are reared by Ken Moffet just up the road, and are superb in taste and texture); don't miss the seafood cookery, such as fried skate with chilli jam, and above all don't miss the desserts, at which Maguire has no peer in the entire country: vanilla panna cotta is decadently light; pavlova with passion fruit curd a thrill of sweet flavours. Sunday lunch is one of the great bargains, and to make the most of the trip to Blacklion, do book one of the simple rooms and treat yourself.

(Blacklion, Co Cavan, Tel: (072) 53022 Fax: 53404, Open D and Sun L, L€€, D€€, Accommodation €€)

To-die-for desserts

Five favourites from MacNean Bistro:

COCONUT AND VANILLA CRÈME BRÛLÉE
With homemade honeycomb ice cream

CHOCOLATE TIRAMISU
With a coffee crème anglaise and white chocolate ice cream

VANILLA AND RUM PANNA COTTA
With poached strawberries and fruit of the forest ice cream

ICED HAZELNUT NOUGAT
With a brunoise of citrus and passion fruit and praline ice cream

VALRHONA CHOCOLATE PLATE
Chocolate fondant, white and dark chocolate sorbet, delice of chocolate, deep-fried beignet of chocolate

North Clare: eating

The cutting-edge cook is Neville Fitzpatrick at **Liscannor's** simple and buzzy **The Mermaid,** where Kathi Marr runs a great room and where the chef and his team produce food that hits every pleasure spot: superlative crab Florentine; brilliant sea bass with spinach and orange; surprisingly delicate swordfish with lime and pepper, served with some of the best mashed potatoes you can eat in Ireland. Don't miss the French beers. (Tel: (065) 7081076, themermaid@ireland.com, Open D, D€€)

Further north, in **Doolin,** the **Doolin Café,** (Tel: (065) 707 4795 Open L&D, L€, D€€) **Doolin Crafts Gallery,** (Tel: (065) 707 4309, Open L, L€), **Cullinan's** (Tel: (065) 707 4183, Open D, D€€) and **The Lazy Lobster** (Tel: (065) 707 4390, Open D,

D€€) all offer well-realised, personal food in simple and laid-back settings and all have their champions, but do note that the village can be absolutely thronged in summer.

In **Lisdoonvarna,** various members of the Sheedy family run both **Sheedy's Spa Hotel** (Tel: (065) 707 4026, Fax: 707 4555, sheedys@gofree.indigo.ie, Open L&D, L€, D€€, Rooms €€€) and **Ballinalacken Castle,** (Tel: (065) 707 4025, ballinalackencastle@eircom.net, Open D, D€€) a couple of miles outside the town as you drive to the coast. The cooking in both is ambitious and professional, though the rooms don't really have that holiday joie de vivre one wants when on holiday in Clare.

In **Lahinch,** Paul and Theresa O'Brien have run the **Barrtrá Seafood Restaurant** with great distinction for more than a decade. Lovely seafood

cookery in a charming, domestic setting, and amazing views across Liscannor Bay.
(Tel: (065) 708 1280, barrtra@iol.ie, Open D, D€€)

● **Byrne's** in **Ennistymon** is a swish modern room that seems to have been transplanted from some metropolis. Unlike other Clare restaurants they use very little local produce, and the food is determinedly modern – wonton Caesar salad; roast and braised lamb shank.
(Main St, Tel: (065) 707 2103 Open D, D€€.
byrnesennistymon@eircom.net)

● In **Kilfenora,** the choice is always **Vaughan's Pub,** where the bar food has true ambition and true flavours, thanks to the use of whatever organic ingredients they can get: this is smart food. Good pints and music sessions here also, and Kilfenora is a darling little village.
(Tel: (065) 708 8004, Open L& early D, L€, D€)

● Locals in and around **Corofin** head for the intimate **Le Catelinais** where Siobhan O'Connor and Yanne

Lecathelinais offer good value comfort food such as chicken satay with rice; fillet of salmon with lemon beurre blanc.
(Tel: (065) 683 7425, Open D, D€€)

● The ever-popular little town of **Ballyvaughan** offers a host of good places. In **The Whitethorn,** which also boasts a super craft shop and exhibition space, John and Sarah McDonnell cook very true, tasty, generous food, and eating lunch outside, enjoying the view across Galway Bay, is a true treat.
Ballyvaughan, Tel: (065) 707 7044, Open L, L€. In the town, Catherine O'Brien's lovely tea rooms, **An Fear Gorta,** is not to be missed: truly sublime baking and a balmy bohemian ambience in a beautiful garden.
(Ballyvaughan, Tel: (065) 707 7023, Open daily, €) Both **Hyland's Hotel** (Tel: (065) 707 7037, Open L&D, L€, D€€) and **Monk's Bar** (Tel: (065) 707 7059, Open L&D, L€, D€€) are good places for simple chowders and other fish and shellfish dishes, and **The Tea Junction Café** is great for late breakfasts.
(Tel: (065) 707 7289, Open daily, Meals €)

South Clare: eating

● Harry McKeogh's **Cherry Tree Restaurant,** right on the border between Clare and Tipperary, is the hot destination in south Clare. McKeogh has a great room and a great team of young locals and the food is sublime, with classic signature dishes such as asparagus bundles with truffle oil; roast wild salmon with salsa verde; dry aged sirloin of beef, and benchmark desserts. Truly one of the don't-miss destinations right now. (Lakeside, Ballina, Killaloe, Co Clare, Tel: (061) 375688 Fax: 375689, Open D, D€€)

● The other hot shot in the region is Patricia Cahill's **Flappers Restaurant,** on the main street in Tulla. Ms Cahill is a great cook with a feminine touch who can produce food that is robust yet subtle. Great service and great value square the circle on a great place. (Main St, Tulla, Co Clare, Tel: (065) 683 5711, Open L&D, L€, D€€)

● Just outside **Milltown Malbay,** locals love the particularity and care which Rita Meade lavishes on both her food and her guests in **Berry Lodge.** Excellent, domestic cooking has won a devoted local following who are extra-appreciative of the lodge. (Annagh, Milltown Malbay, Co Clare, Tel: (065) 708 7022 Fax: 708 7011, ritameade@esatclear.ie, berrylodge.com, Open D, & Sun L, D€€)

● And on the coast road. Tom and Bernadette Hamilton's **Black Oak Restaurant,** in a striking building overlooking the sea, offers classical, deftly executed and properly served cooking which you never tire of: rack of lamb with colcannon; their trademark house salad, seafood pot; aubergine bake. (Rineen, Milltown Malbay, Co Clare, Tel: (065) 708 4408, Open D, D€€)

South Clare

In **Ennis,** Ireland's information age town, the favourite local places for lunch are **Henry's Deli,** now moved to a smart new room at the Abbey Street car park, where Henry Benagh packs 'em in for his trademark hot sandwiches and the best coffee and ice cream in town. (Riverside House, Abbey St Car Park, Ennis, Tel: (065) 682 2848. Open L, L€) Also popular, especially for their trademark salads, is Anne Leyden's **Ennis Gourmet Store,** at the top of the town on Barrack Street. This is also a great shop where you will find the best foods of the county: see the shoppers' guide for full details. (1 Barrack St, Tel: (065) 684 3314, gourmetstore@eircom.net Open L, L€) Just across from the Gourmet store is **La Café des Gourmets,** run by partners of the Gourmet store, with good salads and charcuterie plates, good drinks and real ice cream. Both shops have excellent wines for sale. (The Square, Barrack St, Ennis Tel: (065) 684 3314, Open L, L€) The town's swishest room is the gorgeous **Town Hall Café,** on O'Connell Street, which has some nice modern cooking and some extremely nice art works. (O'Connell St, Tel: (065) 682 8127 oghotel@iol.ie Open L&D, L€€, D€€) The leading ethnic choice is the pricey-but-worth-it **Jasmine Palace,** on Barrack Street. (Tel: (065) 6868188, Open L&D, L€€, D€€) In the curiously-named **Halpino's** Derek Halpin and his chef, Nathan Brook, offer

WHERE TO STAY

• One of our favourite B&B's has always been Mary Kelleher's **Fergus View**, just south of the Burren in **Kilnaboy,** a few miles from Corofin. Some folk dislike the fact that the rooms are small, but we think that just reinforces the feeling of cosy comfort which is what this house is all about. Mrs Kelleher is also a fine, interested cook, and her dinners are treats of lush, domestic cooking. (Kilnaboy, Corofin, Tel: (065) 683 7606, Fax: 683 7182 deckell@indigo.ie, rates €€)

• Closer to Lake Inchiquin in **Corofin** is one of the quintessential country houses: Jim and Bernadette Robson's spiffing **Clifden House**. This is one of the great country houses, with owners as singular and idiosyncratic as the house itself. If you value the unexpected, the out-of-step and out-of-time, then Clifden is for you. (Corofin, Co Clare, Tel & Fax: (065) 683 7692, Rates €€)

South Clare

modern, ambitious cooking: smoked salmon and avocado wonton with citrus dressing; loin of lamb with ragoût of peppers and spiced couscous; duck breast with sesame spaghetti. 7 High St, Ennis, Tel: (065) 684 0011, Fax: 684 0022, halpinosrestaurant@eircom.net, halpinos.com, Open D, D€€. For good fresh fish, then **McCanny's** fish restaurant on Salthouse Lane is a popular choice, and the quality of fish is always high, the menu reassuringly concise, the room reassuringly busy.
(17-18 Salthouse Lane, Tel: (065) 682 3686, Open L & D, L€, D€€)

● Deep down south, **Morrissey's** pub in **Doonbeg** is practically a local legend for finger lickin' seafood cookery – jumbo prawns in garlic butter; seafood platter; pan-fried plaice, and lots of other popular foods which they cook with verve. Do note that it gets very, very busy during the season, so get here early. (Doonbeg, Tel: (065) 905 5304, Open L&D, L€, D€€)

● Down in **Kilkee,** Imelda Bourke's **The Pantry** is the local choice for foods both to eat in – in the restaurant – and to take away, from The Pantry Shop, which makes it a big hit with folk who holiday down here: lovely chowder; good pastas; Carrigaholt mussels; a good daily fish dish. (O'Curry St, Kilkee, Tel: (065) 905 6576, Open B, L & D, B€, L€, D€€)

WHERE TO STAY

• Rita Meade offers B&B in **Berry Lodge**, her restaurant and cookery school near to **Miltown Malbay**. (see page 22).

• An interesting new find is **Drumcreehy House**, Bernadette and Armin Greskes' B&B, where the views and the fine breakfasts are splendid. (Tel: (065) 7077377 b&b@drumcreehyhouse.com Rates €€)

• In **Ballyvaughan**, the rooms in **Hylands Hotel** are comfortable, especially the newer ones at the rere. (see page 21, Rates €€€)

NOTE:
**If you are taking the tour of the bear caves at Aillwee Caves, make sure to allow yourself time to have something to eat in the café.
Most food in exhibition spaces is poor, but this is an exception, and the care they take comes through in good, enjoyable food. The tour itself is brilliant.**

Cork city restaurants

The most dazzling cooking in Cork city comes from Mercy Fenton, in the grand and lovely Jacob's on the Mall, on South Mall, and from Denis Cotter of Café Paradiso, on the Western Road, the finest vegetarian cook in these islands.

● In **Jacobs,** Ms Fenton marries a subtle, understated technique with a profound appreciation of the logic of flavour, to produce some of the most sublime food being cooked in the country, never mind the city: simple things such as onion and cider soup; beautifully structured main courses such as seatrout with melted tomatoes, roast fennel and potato rösti, great signature desserts such as falling chocolate cake. Great service makes this a super room for both dating and entertaining.
(30a South Mall, Cork, Tel: (021) 425 1530, Fax: (021) 425 1531, kingsley@eircom.net, Open L&D, L€€, D€€€)

Where to stay in Cork City:

We reckon the breakfast served in Angela Hegarty's town house, 7 North Mall, is amongst the best in the country. It's not profuse: it's just beautifully judged and uses the best ingredients you can buy and cooks them beautifully. A great cult address, and just a short stroll from the city centre. Say hello to the ambassador as you pass on the stairs.
(7 North Mall, Cork, Tel: (021) 439 7191, Fax: 430 0811, sevennorthmall@eircom.net, Rates €€)
Out on the Western Road, there are a zillion B&B's: head straight for Hansi Lucey's Garnish House (yellow sign, right hand side) and you will be a happy bunny, for this lady and her team look after you just the way you like to be looked after. Bliss.
(Western Rd, Cork, Tel: 427 5111, Fax: 427 3872, garnish@iol.ie, garnish.com, Rates €€)

Cork City

CHEF'S PASSIONS

Denis Cotter, Café Paradiso

'The two dishes I most love to cook are peperonata and risotto. I love the way peperonata cooks, when you get it right. If you don't boil it, but simmer it perfectly, it sweetens up, and I love the smell of it cooking.

Risotto is slow, rhythmic and relaxing to cook, which goes against the grain with what goes on in a restaurant.

'The dishes I often hate to cook in the restaurant are fresh pasta and the stir fry. I enjoy making the dishes themselves, they're great fun to make, but there will always be a dish on the menu which nervous customers will hit on, and for me that will be fresh pasta and the stir fry, and you have to spend your night focusing on one dish, while the rest of the food is ignored. It's my version of the steak thing, and it drives me crazy.'

● In **Café Paradiso,** Denis Cotter turns culinary rules on their head: he doesn't cook meat, yet at any given time, 90% of his customers will be carnivores, and the majority of those customers are women. Vegetarianism isn't in it: this is simply superlative cooking from an uninhibitedly imaginative chef who makes dishes – such as baked Portobello mushroom with Cashel Blue cheese, pecan crumbs and sage and smoked paprika roll – that other chefs simply would never dream of composing. The room has a gorgeous bohemianism, worthy of Cork's student quarter, and great service, sounds and wine list. A unique place. (16 Lancaster Quay, Western Rd, Cork, Tel: (021) 427 7939, Fax: 430 7469, Open L&D, L€, D€€)

● Seamus O'Connell is back in the kitchens of **The Ivory Tower,** upstairs on Princes Street, after a spell spent opening Pi, on Washington Street. On song, Mr O'Connell's cooking is outstanding, and quite unlike anyone else's way of combining and presenting food. He is a true culinary polymath, and dinner here is a walk on the wildside, but for some this wildside is too extreme, and the casualness of service and décor offers no chintzy comfort. (The Ivory Tower, The Exchange Buildings, 35 Princes Street, Tel: (021) 427 4665. Open D, D€€)

● Away from the cutting edge, Cork city also offers several superlative restaurants where stylish comfort food is done as good as it can be. **Jacques,** on Phoenix Street just beside the post office, which the Barry sisters have been running for more than two decades, and where chef Eileen Carey has been cooking for 15 years, is still one of the city's favourite places for great food: punchy scallops and Clonakilty black pudding with tomato vinaigrette; bistro classics such as sirloin steak with deep-fried onions, sauté potatoes and café de paris butter. The room has great atmosphere,and value for money is very keen, and check out the super-enthusiastic wine list!
(Phoenix St, Cork, Tel: (021) 427 7387, Fax: 427 0634, Open L&D, L€, D€€)

● Another informal yet smart room is **No 5 Fenns Quay,** at the back of the courthouse, a great favourite with Cork folk. Everyone comes here for food that is logical, flavourful and fun: Hederman's salmon with crushed potato and cucumber salad; guinea fowl with bacon mash; tarte tatin with caramel ice cream. The smallness of the room makes it very cosy and intimate.
(5 Fenn's Quay, Cork, Tel: (021) 427 9527, Open daily till 10pm, L€, D€€)

A JACQUES CLASSIC:

'We've had roast duck on the menu for the last 21 years, and we just haven't been able to stop serving it. Once we took it off for a full year, and we nearly had people walking out.
'We always served it roasted, with a potato and apricot stuffing and apricot and tamarind sauce - though the tamarind only came along about fifteen year's ago.
'This year, we've actually re-jigged it, and now as well as roasting the duck, we also offer the breast meat, cooked to order, with the same sauce, so people can order it rare if they want.
'Another dish that has come back onto our menu due to customer demand is Seafood barquette: a pastry boat, filled with prawns, grilled, with a cream sauce. It was on the menu 21 years ago. So we call it a Jacques Classic.' – Jacqueline Barry

Cork City

● It may be a pity that the beautiful **Crawford Gallery Cafe** in Emmet Place is not open for dinner, but the day-time food here makes this a true favourite amongst locals. The Crawford is a city-branch of the Ballymaloe empire, and the cooking wears the same profound modesty and deliciousness which is the Ballymaloe signature. Give us the Ballycotton mackerel and the Dingle pie (above all the Dingle pie) and the biscuits and the bakewell and we are as happy as can be. Crawford Gallery, Emmet Place, (Tel: (021) 427 4415, Open L, L€)

● We also like the artistic atmosphere in the **Farmgate Café,** in the English Market, where Kay Harte and her team cook true Cork food for Cork folk: most of the ingredients they use are sourced right here in the market, then cooked that day. Charming service, great value, and an essential part of any market trawl. (Old English Market, Princes St, Cork, Tel: (021) 427 8134, Fax: 427 8134, Open L, L€)

● **Isaac's** is an institution at this stage of its life, and it's a lovely room on MacCurtain St, north of the river, just as charming as ever and co-owner Canice Sharkey's food is as snappy and tasty as it comes: good stews – very good stews – and pastas; excellent shellfish, moreish desserts make for simple, timeless, elegant food. (48 MacCurtain St, Cork, Tel: (021) 450 3805, Fax: 455 1348, isaacs@iol.ie Open L&D, L€, D€€)

● **Wild Ways** is a new coffee bar and food-to-go emporium with the ambition of using exclusively organic ingredients. So organic tea and toast, to begin the day, and then lots of zesty organic rolls and wraps for lunch. You can order on-line from www.wildways.net, and pick up from their location in central Cork. Nice staff, and rather fetching crockery. (21 Princes St, Cork, wildways.net, open daily, €)

● A pair of Cork places owned by a team are Bourke & Foyle's **Bodega** and **Coal Quay Café,** adjacent to each other on Cornmarket Street. These are stylish, swish rooms, with straightforward, modern cooking, but what we like about them is the energy of the two places.

(Bodega, 46-49 Cornmarket St, Cork, Tel: (021) 427 2878. Open daily, €€)
(Coal Quay Café, Cornmarket Street, Cork Tel: (021) 427 2880 Open D, D€€)

● There is energy and great ambient sounds in the super-stylish **Pi,** across from the courthouse on Washington Street, and like everyone else we lurve this great room, and wait to see how the food evolves after they have finished a present series of changes. (Courthouse Chambers, Washington St, Cork, Tel: (021) 422 2860, Open L&D, L€, D€-€€)

● **Lovett's** is another restaurant which is undergoing changes, and we look forward to what Marie Harding, a fine cook, will weave out of the new make-over on this southside institution. (Churchyard Lane, off Well Rd, Douglas, Cork, Tel: (021) 429 4909, Fax: 429 4024, lovetts@indigo.ie, Open L&D, L€-€€, D€€)

● And you want to be a true Corkonian? Then head down to **Jackie Lennox's Chipper** on the Bandon Road, join the queue, and eat the chips the good folk of Cork have been scoffing since 1952, maybe with a potato pie. Chips and potato pie: that's your starch sorted for the week, then. (137 Bandon Rd, Cork, Tel: (021) 431 6118 Meals €)

REAL FOOD

The Farmgate Café in the English Market in Cork city centre is a true market café: the kitchen uses ingredients bought in the market downstairs to bring alive the authentic flavours of those dishes regarded as amongst the finest from Ireland's traditional cuisine.
Here is the roll call of the traditional Irish dishes on offer in the Farmgate:

▪ TRIPE & DRISHEEN
Not for the faint-hearted

▪ IRISH STEW
The original of all the daubes

▪ LAMBS LIVER & BACON
Offal lovers' heaven

▪ SHEPHERD'S PIE
Children's favourite

▪ TRADITIONAL IRISH BREAKFAST
Using Clonakilty Black Pudding and Sausages.
Cholesterol city

▪ CLONAKILTY PUDDING SAVOURY TART
Agrestic magnificence

East Cork

● The legendary Ballymaloe House is most everyone's destination address in East Cork, but before you reach Ballymaloe, pause for a while in the little village of Cloyne, step into a smart little pub called **The Cross of Cloyne,** order dinner, and let Colm Falvey knock your socks off with some fantastic cooking. The Cross is the big hit of this area, and Falvey's cooking shows just why: he deals with flavours like a maestro, yet his food is modest and devoted to enjoyment, revealing the time he spent at the stoves in Ballymaloe: cassoulet of Cuddigan's lamb; plaice with roasted field mushrooms; Ballycotton mackerel with a herb butter.
(Cloyne, nr Midleton, Tel: (021) 465 2401, Fax: 465 2401, Open Dinner, D€€)

● And there is another nice surprise before you get to Ballymaloe: several hundred yards before the house you will find Geraldine O'Brien's lovely country house, **Barnabrow** (see Where To Stay, right) guests can eat in the Mor Chluna restaurant. (Cloyne, Tel: (021) 465 2534, barnabrow@eircom.net, barnabrowhouse.com, Open D, D€€)

WHERE TO STAY

■ **The B's have it: Ballymaloe and Barnabrow are great east Cork houses, and Ballymakeigh wins a constant stream of admirers for Margaret Browne's hospitality.**

■ **Barnabrow is a romantic, loveable house, and popular with wedding parties for that very reason.
(Cloyne, Midleton, Tel: (021) 465 2534, barnabrow@eircom.net, Rates €€)**

■ **Ballymaloe House is modest (many folk who come here for the first time are shocked at its small size) but it has been the most important address in the history of modern Irish food. Don't expect slickness, by the way: it's country simplicity defined, so no CNN, thank heavens. (Shanagarry, Midleton, Tel: (021) 465 2531, Fax: 465 2021, res@ballymaloe.ie, ballymaloe.ie, Rates €€€)**

Myrtle Allen of **Ballymaloe House** is not just one of the great Irish cooks, she is also one of the great Irish modernists, and one of the great Irish iconoclasts. The food here is always enjoyable, the atmosphere inimitable, the graciousness of the rooms (and the amazing art collection) always a delight. (See left for details.)

In Midleton, Marog O'Brien continues to cook and serve excellent country cooking in **The Farm Gate,** a cosy, comfy restaurant which locals adore. "You'd get a nice piece of liver, or fresh fish, perfectly cooked," they will tell you. We'll have one of each please, Marog. (Coolbawn, Midleton, Tel: (021) 4632771, Open L & D at weekends, L€, D€€)

In Killeagh, heading eastwards on the N25, Margaret Browne made her name with **Ballymakeigh House**, a fine farmhouse B&B, but she has now opened **Browne's** restaurant, on the main N25 a few miles from Killeagh, with great success. We don't know how she manages to run two businesses several miles apart, but folk just love them both and write to us at the Bridgestone guides with amazing frequency to tell us. The food is nice and homely, simple and well-achieved, great for kids. (Killeagh, Tel: (024) 95184, Open L&D, L€, D€)

WHERE TO STAY

■ The cult address in this neck of the woods is Beth Hallinan's Rathcoursey House, on the East Ferry road: we want the room with the log fire and the antler's head gazing down at you as you soak, anticipating Ms Hallinan's fine country house dinner. (Ballinacurra, Nr Midleton, Tel: (021) 461 3418, Fax: 461 3393 beth@rathcoursey.com, rathcoursey.com, Rates €€)

■ Youghal, on the edge of the county, is home to the legendary Aherne's: beautiful bar, famous fish restaurant and excellent rooms. The Fitzgibbon family have nothing to learn about the hospitality and cooking businesses, but continue to learn they do, improving their pristine operation each and every year. The bar food, incidentally, is amongst the best you can eat, but then most everything here is benchmark. (163 North Main St, Youghal, Tel: (024) 92424, Fax: 93633, ahernes@eircom.net, ahernes.com, Rates €€€)

North Cork

Here be great country houses: Assolas House in Kanturk and Longueville House in Mallow offer the most exciting, cutting-edge cookery found in any Irish country house, whilst Ballyvolane House in Castlelyons is one of the dreamiest country house experiences you can enjoy.

● Hazel and Joe Bourke run **Assolas House,** a petite Queen Anne house, which feels like a planet unto itself. This peaceful perfection is echoed by Hazel Bourke's cookery, which is meticulous and magnificent and has a style all of its own; sometimes the tastes are so pure and unmediated, it's as if the food has been transformed, rather then cooked. Simple brilliance and brilliant simplicity. An unmissable address. (Kanturk, Co Cork Tel: (029) 50015, Fax:60795, assolas@eircom.net, assolas.com, Rates €€€)

● William O'Callaghan's cooking in **Longueville House,** only a few miles east of Assolas, is regarded by many food lovers as perhaps the finest in Ireland.

Restaurants

• In Fermoy, the destination address has always been Rodolphe and Noelle Semeria's quirky La Bigoudenne, which will soon be back in the town after a temporary shift to their house in Conna. Simple and enjoyable cooking in a simple room – and a splendid Gallic insouciance that we just love. At lunchtime, don't miss their fantastic crepes: buckwheat and blue cheese will cure all ills and get you on the road again. (28 McCurtain St, Fermoy, Co Cork, Tel: (025) 32832, Open L&D, L€, D€€)

What we admire about Mr O'Callaghan's cooking is the fact that he is a true countryman: he understands and appreciates every nuance of his ingredients, and then cooks them with abiding and consummate skill. There is nothing he can't bring his magic to, and he has the benefit of not just a truly splendid country house in which to work, but also the fact that the O'Callaghan family have hospitality bred into the bone, and it shows in the superhuman generosity they exhibit. Fabulous. Mallow, Co Cork, Tel: (022) 47156, Fax: 47459, info@longuevillehouse.ie, longuevillehouse.ie, Open D, D€€€, Accommodation rates €€€.

● It might seem a more modest place by comparison, but Merrie and Jeremy Green's **Ballyvolane House** is one of the peachiest country houses you can find, and they succeed because the attention paid to detail here is paid to each and every element of this handsome house and its table. The cooking is splendid, the companionship around the big dining room table brought to a pitch by people having the time of their lives. Fabulous, and you have always wanted to stay someplace run by a lady called Merrie, haven't you?
(Castlelyons, Fermoy, Co Cork, Tel: (025) 36349, Fax: (025) 36781, info@ballyvolanehouse.ie, ballyvolanehouse.ie, Rates €€€)

• In Mitchelstown, the key address is O'Callaghan's deli and café, just near to the junction and traffic lights on Cork Street at the northern end of the town. Lovely baking, excellent comforting and generous lunches, and sheer hard work and dedication have made Mary and Pat's deli the destination for food lovers in Mitchelstown. They also cook excellent food-to-go for folk with no time to spend in the kitchen. A brilliant on-the-road stop also.
(19-29 Lower Cork St, Mitchelstown, Tel; (025) 24657, Open daily, L€)

West Cork food route

A Westward Journey, from Kinsale through to Ballylickey, calling in on Kilbrittain, Butlerstown, Clonakilty, Timoleague, Roscarbery, Glandore, Castletownshend, Skibbereen, Baltimore, Ballydehob, Schull, Crookhaven, Durrus, and Bantry. Follow the arrows (⇨) on these pages to take you West.

KINSALE

● Every day at the **Fishy Fishy Café** in Kinsale, Martin and Marie Shanahan actually turn away as many customers as they can manage to serve. Everyone who comes to pretty Kinsale wants to eat in the Fishy Fishy, and with good reason: the fishy fishy cookery is as good as it gets: casserole of monkfish and tiger prawns in a tarragon cream; roast fillet of hake with Asian butter; warm salad of chilli squid with chickpeas. The food is devastatingly delicious, the atmosphere up to 90°. Who cares about waiting in the queue: it's worth it.
(Fishy Fishy. Guardwell, Kinsale, Co Cork, Tel: (021) 477 4453, Open daily, L€)

● Our favourite place to stay in town is just up the hill from the Fishy Fishy. Maeve Coakley has created the most beautiful space in **Blindgate House,** a real style-lover's destination. This is serene, elegant comfort at its best, the breakfasts are fantastic, and we could look at the art works all day long: Blindgate is where you want to be.
(Blindgate House, Kinsale, Co Cork
info@blindgatehouse.com Tel: (021) 477 7858, Fax: 477 7868, Rates €€)

West Cork food route

● There is also good accommodation in **The Old Bankhouse** in the centre of town, where Michael Reise runs a superbly professional little hotel. (11 Pearse St, Kinsale, Co Cork, Tel: (021) 477 4075, Fax: 477, 4296, oldbank@indigo.ie, Rates €€)

● For generous, unpretentious food, in an eternally buzzy atmosphere, then try **Man Friday,** up the hill. Scilly, Kinsale, (Tel: (021) 477 2260, Fax: 477 2262, Open D, D€)

● In the town, **Max's Wine Bar** and **Crackpots Restaurant** are the most interesting places to eat amongst the numerous choices. (Max's, Main St, Tel: (021) 477 2443, Open L & D, L€, D€€) (Crackpots, Cork St, crackpts@iol.ie, Tel: (021) 477 2847. Open D & Sun L, D€€)

⇨ KILBRITTAIN

● **Casino House** is the destination address here, for Michael Relja's excellent cooking draws in food lovers for miles around. The restaurant is a simply darling space, and the serious – but not too serious – food is technically well-accomplished and well-considered, and is amongst the best cooking in West Cork. (Coolmain Bay, Kilbrittain, Co Cork, Tel: (023) 49944, chouse@eircom.net, Open D, D & Sun L, D€€, L€€)

FISHY DISHIES

Martin Shanahan, of Fishy Fishy Café, names his top Six Most Popular Dishes of the Summer:

■ **GRILLED WHOLE PRAWNS**
Served in the shell with lemon, garlic and sweet chili sauce

■ **COLD SEAFOOD PLATTER**
With salmon, prawns, mussels, oyster, crab & smoked salmon

■ **CRAB CLAWS**
in Asian butter

■ **ROAST FILLET OF HAKE**
With buttered new potatoes, tomato salsa, basil dressing

■ **RED GURNARD**
Pan fried on a bed of root vegetable purée, lemon butter sauce

■ **WARM SALAD OF SQUID**
With pickled ginger, sesame seeds and spring onion

West Cork food route

⇨ BUTLERSTOWN

● Otto Kunze is one of the cult figures of Irish food, a pioneer of organic foods, and one of the great cooks and teachers. You will need to be a party of folk to book his restaurant in **Otto's Creative Cuisine**, so gather all your friends and head down to this unique place. Otto's is a restaurant and cookery school with accommodation for cookery students, and the food is superlative, most of it grown and raised by Otto and Hilda themselves. Dunworley, Butlerstown, Bandon, Tel: (023) 40461, Fax: 40482, ottokunze@eircom.net, ottos-creative-catering.com

● Not too far away, we love the restrained, minimalist perfection of **Butlerstown House,** one of the finest Georgian houses you can stay in anywhere in Ireland. This is a dream destination for style lovers. Butlerstown, Bandon, Tel: (023) 40137, butlerstownhouse.com, mail@butlerstownhouse.com, Rates €€.

⇨ TIMOLEAGUE

● **Lettercollum House** has been one of the benchmark addresses in West Cork for years, but these days it caters solely for groups and gatherings who wish to book the house, and have Con McLoughlin and Karen Austin cook for them. There is no better reason to organise a gathering of the tribe, for Con and Karen are brilliant cooks, truly original culinary talents whose food is spontaneous and utterly true. If we were having a convocation of all the McKennas, *(unlikely, Ed)* then believe us, this would be the first choice resort. (Timoleague, Tel: (023) 4625, conmac@iol.ie, lettercollum.ie)

⇨ CLONAKILTY

● **Fionnuala's Little Italian Restaurant** is everyone's book-it! destination in 'Clon (as the locals call it). Truthfully, the cooking is

West Cork food route

more Fionnuala than Italian, and that is how we, and everyone else, like it, for Fionnuala Harkin is a great hostess, and has a sure touch for accessible, flavourful food, especially her trademark pizzas and lasagnes. Pure fun.
(30 Ashe St, Clonakilty, Co Cork, Tel: (023) 34355, Open D, D€-€€)

● There is also interesting food in **An Sugan,** close to the centre of town. Even though it is a pub, Brenda and Kevin O'Crowley invest a lot of ambition with their food, and locals rate it very highly indeed.
(41 Strand St, Clonakilty, Tel: (023) 33498, Open L&D, L€, D€€)

⇨ **ROSCARBERY**

Detour off the road and head up into the town square in Roscarbery, and you will find one of the great West Cork restaurants.
O'Callaghan-Walshe sounds like a funny name for a place to eat, and it is a funny place to eat, for it's a most curious pub and restaurant. But Sean Kearney knows all about good cooking, and so O'C-W is the hottest place around. If you are really hungry, then order the shellfish platter, which delivers enough shellfish for about four people. Mighty, mighty fun.
(Rosscarbery, Co Cork, Tel: (023) 48125, funfish@indigo.ie, Open D, D€€)

Pig party:

'Never name a pig, because you'll never bring yourself to eat it. If I call them anything, I call my pigs "bacon", and "chop".
'I use the head to make brawn, using the crubeens to make the jelly. I make smoked salami sausages, and terrines with the belly. Liver goes to make the pâté. I salt and smoke the loins and legs to make bacon and ham. The ribs and bones I turn into gravy for the roasts that I make from the leg. I once made a tobacco pouch out of the bladder, but now I'm a non smoker. The kidneys, I keep for myself.'

OTTO KUNZE

West Cork food route

⇨ GLANDORE

● Declan and Ada Hayes beloved **Hayes Bar** is the place to be in Glandore. The care taken with every detail of their food and drink and the affection lavished on this simple pub is inspiring, nothing less. Declan and Ada manage to make everything special, so a lazy lunch with some fine wine sitting outside looking across the harbour is some sort of bliss indeed. You won't forget it. (Glandore, Tel: (028) 33214, Open daily in season, L€)

⇨ CASTLETOWNSHEND

● You need to be sober to navigate Castletownshend, for it has the steepest street in West Cork, and that street has a tree in the middle of it! Locals take all this in their stride, whilst visitors come here to stay in **Bow Hall**, a truly special B&B run with magnificent exuberance by Barbara and Dick Vickery (don't miss the pork and apple breakfast patties), and to eat in **Mary Ann's**, one of the original cult West Cork addresses and, as such, a staple of every guide book you can buy. But, Mary Ann's isn't some tourist facsimile: there is real food here, both in the bar and in the restaurant upstairs and it's a truly beautiful space. (Castletownshend, Tel: (028) 436114, Rates €€. Mary Ann's, Town Square, Castletownshend, Tel: (028) 436146, Open L&D, L€, D€€)

⇨ SKIBBEREEN

● In Skibb, **Kalbo's Bistro** hoovers up all of the local trade thanks to some smart, fun cooking; good potato skins with chili; bruschetta with roasted peppers and cheese; good chunky steaks and home-made burgers; fine desserts such as autumn fruit meringue soufflé. This is nice cooking, and do check out their shop, also, just across the street, for some good breads to take home with you. At the other end of town, **Ty Ar Mor** is a small fish restaurant with a very French focus and the cooking has polish and flavour aplenty, though the room can be a little formal and quiet, so save it for a buzzy weekend night. (Kalbo's Bistro, 48 Nth St, Skibbereen, Tel: (028) 21515, kalbo@eircom.net, Open L&D, L€, D€€. Ty Ar Mor, 46 Bridge St, Tel: (028) 22100, Fax: 22834, tyarmor@iol.ie. Open D, D€€)

● Just around the corner, the wonderful **West Cork Hotel** is run with magnificent élan by John Murphy, and discovering the West Cork for the first time is a dream. There is a lovely dining room with good cooking, and it's a fantastic stop for lunch in the bar. There really is no place quite like this jewel of an hotel. (Ilen St, Skibbereen, Tel: (028) 21277, Fax: 22333 westcorkhotel.com, info@westcorkhotel.com, Rates €€-€€€)

● A few miles westwards on the road, you take the signs for Heir Island, drive down the snaky road to the little ferry, and here begins one of the most extraordinary food adventures in Ireland.
John Desmond and Ellmary Fenton run **Island Cottage Restaurant** on the tiny Heir Island. You take the boat across, walk for 10 minutes up the boreen, then walk into a tiny, single room restaurant which can sit about 20 people. There is no choice with the food, for everyone eats the same dinner, and the food can be nothing less than perfection. Indeed Marcella Hazan, the greatest writer on Italian food and one of the world's greatest cooks, described the food in Island Cottage as the finest she encountered in Ireland – smooth duck liver pâté, magnificent crab risotto, fillet of lamb with gratin dauphinoise, with courgettes with wild mushrooms and a jus of lamb juices, fabulous baked lemon soufflé. If you come to West Cork and don't go to Island Cottage, then you haven't really been to West Cork. (Heir Island, Skibbereen, Tel/Fax: (028) 38102, islandcottage.com, Open D, D€€)

West Cork food route

⇨ **BALTIMORE**

● **The Customs House** restaurant is the second great restaurant icon of West Cork, along with Island Cottage. Sue Holland's fish cookery in these lean, simple rooms has no peer in Ireland, and she matches a total understanding of flavour with inspiring discipline. With Ian Parr manning front of house, this is one of the most thrilling restaurants in Ireland, and simply must not be missed. As well as offering some of the best food in the country, The Customs House is also the best value restaurant, and they play Bill Evans CDs all the time, so jazzers are just blissed out to be here. (Baltimore, Tel: (028) 20200, Open D, D€€)

FISH KNOW HOW
from Ian Parr, The Customs House

'One of the best fish in the ocean is turbot, it's nice on the bone, it's nice off the bone. It's so meaty, it doesn't disintegrate into baby food like it's cousin the brill does unless it's treated carefully.

'Red mullet is a stray character, so we don't always get it, but when we do, we like to roast it on the bone with a socca pancake and tapenade. It's a fish that suits simplicity.

'We love sole, and you just can't improve on treating it with a meunière sauce.

'Cod we salt, in the artisanal way, and we never run out of it. We've been refining the recipe for brandade with our own salted cod for five to six years now, and it's just a question of getting the chemistry right.

'Monkfish would be our least favourite, but it's very versatile, you can do all sorts of things with it. A good sauce will make it, or you can put it on the grill. But look carefully at what you're putting with it, because basically, the sauce supplies the taste.'

West Cork food route

● A little further down the street, Lucy Carey's **The Mews** is another delightful little restaurant, and whilst the cooking is conventional, it is very well done and deservedly popular with the yachting types who pack out Baltimore during the season. **Bushe's Bar,** overlooking the harbour, is our favourite place for a pint and a sandwich.
(The Mews, Baltimore, Tel: (028) 20390, Open D, D€€)

⇨ BALLYDEHOB

● **Annie's** has long been the favourite West Cork restaurant for many folk, and the recent enlargement of the dining room hasn't altered the blissful character of this great institution a jot. Friendly, generous cooking, brilliant service from Annie herself, and do make sure to have a drink in **Levis' Bar,** right across the street.
(Main St, Ballydehob, Tel: (028) 37292, Open Dinner, D€€)

⇨ SCHULL

● Schull has lots of places to eat, with Adéle's and the Courtyard the prime choices for lunch. **Adéle's** is a bakery and restaurant and also has four sweet, simple little rooms at the top of the house, which we love. The baking is superb, the lunches fantastic: great salads; lovely filled ciabatta, and don't even think of leaving before you have had a slice of their famous lemon cake. A real West Cork classic. (Main St, Schull, Tel: (028) 28459, Fax: 28865, adelesrestaurant.com, Open daily L€)

● Denis and Finola Quinlan oversee a shop and bar in **The Courtyard,** and somedays you can find the whole tribe of McKennas in the bar here, parents having the toasted special and a pint of Murphy's, and the kids scoffing the soup of the day. Lovely cooking, and a good shop which sells all the great West Cork foods and their own excellent breads. (Main St, Schull, Tel: (028) 28390, Open L & evenings in summertime, Meals €)

West Cork food route

● For pub food, everyone likes **Hackett's,** whilst **La Coquille** is the best bet in the evenings, for good fresh fish, simply cooked. Don't miss **Brosnan's Fish and Chip Shop,** for they offer real fresh fish – sometimes four or five different types, in a real beer batter, make great chips and do good mushy peas. (Hackett's, Main St, Schull, Tel: (028) 28625, Open L, L€) (La Coquille, Main St, Tel: (028) 28642, Open D, D€€. Brosnan's, Main St, Schull, Open evenings, Meals €)

● A little-known place is **The Barn,** which is hard to find up in Dereenatra, and worth the journey. Ann and Frank open their house and cook enjoyable food for groups; make sure to take some salamis home with you. (Dereenatra, Schull, Tel: (028) 28579, Open D, D€€)

● A beautiful B&B is **Grove House,** on the Colla Road, a colourful, splendid place to stay, run by Billy and Mary O'Shea. Each room is different, and the running of the house is meticulous. (Colla Rd, Schull, Tel: (028) 28067, Fax: 28069, billyoshea@yahoo.com. Rates €€)

⇨ GOLEEN

● Violet Connell's **Fortview House** B&B is loved by everyone who goes through its doors. She has a natural eye for design, and she has made every room comfortable by making them beautiful. As good a cook as she is an interior designer, the breakfasts are legendary. (Gurtyowen, Toormore, Goleen, Tel/Fax: (028) 35324, Rates €€)

⇨ CROOKHAVEN

● **O'Sullivan's Bar** acts like a magnet for visitors to little Crookhaven. It's a smashing pub, but don't overlook the food, which is tasty domestic cooking that suits the place to a T, and which is usually just what you felt like eating. Great young staff are a delight, and it's oh-so-easy for a quick drink here to turn into a lazy, boozy afternoon. There has been a lot of development recently up the hill at the **Barley Cove Beach Hotel,** and this could be a very promising place (Tel: (028) 35234) (O'Sullivan's Bar, Crookhaven, Tel: (028) 35319, Open daily, Meals €)

⇨ DURRUS

● In the village, you will find real Belgian home cooking in **Ivo's Bar,** where Maria Peters and her team produce simple fresh food, and what are simply the best pots of steamed mussels you can eat anywhere in Ireland. (Main St, Durrus, Tel: (027) 61109, Open L&D, L€, D€€)

● A couple of miles down the Goleen Road you find **Blair's Cove**, a beautiful house and restaurant which has the most stunning location imaginable, overlooking Dunmanus Bay. The restaurant here is many people's favourite anywhere in Ireland, and it's a truly beautiful room. The cooking offers a large smorgasbord of starters, good grills from the fire, with local cheeses and desserts to follow. The rooms are particularly stylish and desirable, and staying overnight or longer in Blair's Cove is a real treat. (Durrus, Tel: (027) 61041, blairscove@eircom.net, Open D, D€€€, Room rates €€€)

Bantry Bay mussels and chips!

Maria Peters – what is the secret of your Bantry Bay Mussels?

'It's not a secret! This method is known all over Belgium. I use onions, celery and pepper, bring it to the boil, and add the mussels. It was the way my mother - her mother - her mother cooked them.
'You usually serve them with a dip. We like the mustard sauce, and we use the pots we brought from Belgium to serve them in. If you gave a Belgium a *plate* of mussels he'd say - "Where's the rest of them!"'

West Cork food route

⇨ BANTRY

● Three buzzy places in Bantry: For excellent fish cookery, **O'Connor's Seafood Restaurant** in the centre of town is the place to go. Mark O'Connor raises the standards here with each passing year. The Square, Bantry, Tel: (027) 50221, oconnorseafood@yahoo.com, Open D, D€€. Just opposite the SuperValu, Marjorie Kelly cooks seriously delicious modern food in **The Pantry,** a tiny upstairs room which gets packed out with locals at lunchtime. This is mighty cooking with great style. New St, Bantry, Tel: (027) 52181, Open L, D L€, D€. For fine, generous, flavoursome food in one of the town's pubs, then Maurice and Colette O'Donovan are the standard bearers with their cooking in **The Snug,** just as you come into town going westwards. This is real cooking from a serious kitchen.
(The Quay, Bantry, Tel: (027) 50057, Open L, L€)

⇨ BALLYLICKEY

● **Sea View House Hotel** is, for many people, the hotel of their dreams. Kathleen O'Sullivan runs a wonderfully hospitable place, whose style has nothing to do with fad or fashion. Ms O'Sullivan simply does things right, and everything here is founded on hospitality and looking after their guests as well as they possibly can.
(Ballylickey, Bantry, Tel: (027) 50462, Fax: 51555, seaviewhousehotel@eircom.net, Open D, D€€€. Accommodation rates €€€)

● A few miles away, at **Larchwood House**, the cooking in Aidan and Sheila Vaughan's is the best in the area. Mrs Vaughan is a very, very good cook with a style that balances trencherman portions with deft, feminine execution, and everything she cooks is superbly understood. The rooms make it a great overnight place, and the garden is there to be explored in the morning.
(Pearson's Bridge, Tel: (027) 66181, Open D, D€€, Room Rates €€)

Donegal North

THE FAR PENINSULAS

Linger on an itinerary around the northern peninsulas of Donegal for a few days, and you not only avoid the fact that the county is virtually a building site, but you also come to understand the bewitching beauty that makes so many people want to come here.

● On the Inishowen peninsula, the inimitable **Corncrake Restaurant** in Carndonagh ('Carn to you) is one of the best-loved dining rooms in the country. So, what's to love? Well, one room, two girls (Noirín and Brid) and a host of benchmark dishes: crab vinaigrette with its toothy mix of capers, gherkins and parsley; superb mature cheddar and chive soufflé; nettle and fresh herb soup; duck confit with hoisin; chicken with tarragon butter; rack of lamb with Puy lentils; wild salmon with foaming hollandaise. Tasty food, as the professionals say, and the sweet baking is stratospheric, especially the rhubarb ice cream and their trademark orange panna cotta. It's also virtually impossible to pay much more than £20 for dinner. (Carndonagh, Tel: (077) 74534. Open D, D€€)

● On the east of the peninsula, **Kealys Seafood Bar** of Greencastle is the food lover's destination. Everything about this splendid seafood restaurant gladdens the heart: the sureness of the food (it's the sort of place you order fritto misto with confidence), the affability of the staff, the carefree nature of the room and the bar. Don't miss it for benchmark seafood cooking. (Greencastle, Tel/Fax: (077) 81010, kealys@iol.ie, Open L&D, L€, D€€)

● And just further north in Culdaff, **McGroary's** is a local favourite for well-achieved cooking, good bar food and comfortable rooms. The pub is highly regarded for its traditional music sessions. (Culdaff, Tel: (077) 79104, Open L&D, L€, D€€, Accommodation rates €€)

North Donegal

● Another good stop is the charming **Grianan Ailigh** restaurant, at Burt, as you go south to Letterkenny, where Willie Holmes has made a very interesting restaurant out of an old Church of Ireland church. Very popular with locals and very busy in the season. If you stop in Letterkenny, then follow the locals to **The Metropolitan,** an enormous pile of a place at the bottom of the Main Street which draws in all the local business for tasty and ambitious bar food. (106 Lr Main St, Letterkenny, Tel: (074) 20800, Fax: 20803, Open Bar Food L, Restaurant D, L€, D€€)

● In Dunfanaghy, close to Horn Head, the big local success story has been **The Mill Restaurant,** where Susan and Derek Alcorn are producing fantastic food and where the rooms are truly stylish. The setting is idyllic – book a room looking out over New Lake – and the food has a verve and succulence which is beguiling. A brilliant base for exploring the north west of the county. (Figart, Dunfanaghy, Tel/Fax: (074) 36985, Open D, D€€. Accommodation rates €€)

Where to stay:

• The best place to stay on Inishowen is in the extra-comfortable Rossaor House, in Ballyliffin, where Brian and Anne Harkin run a supremely comfy B&B, but if you are en-famille, then do rent one of their excellent self-catering cottages, just up the hill: these are very good indeed. (Ballyliffin, Inishowen, Tel & Fax: (077) 76498, rossaor@gofree.indigo.ie Rates: €€)

• On the Fanad peninsula, everyone heads to Croaghross, at Portsalon. Why? Well, to walk the strand, which is one of the most idyllic stretches of white sand found anywhere in Ireland, and to eat the delicious food and chill out in the comfort zone of John and Kay Deane's lovely house. Great cooking, lovely wines, keen prices, and all round salvation, frankly. (Portsalon, Letterkenny, Tel/Fax: (074) 59548, jkdeane@croaghross.com croaghross.com, Rates €€)

• There is interesting and good value accommodation also at The Mill House, at Corcreggan, just a few miles west of Dunfanaghy, where Brendan Rohan has developed an interesting complex: check out that old railway carriage! (Corcreggan, Dunfanaghy, Tel: (074) 36900, Rates €€, themillhouse@eircom.net

Donegal South

The best place to eat in Donegal town is in **McGroarty's Pub,** at the upper side of the Diamond, where Stella's cooking offers really rather superior pub food, including good pub food for vegetarians.
(The Diamond, Donegal, Tel: (073) 21049, Open daily, L€)

Otherwise, head west, to Dunkineely, where

Castlemurray House has been a beacon of good food for a decade. Some years back, Claire and Thierry Delcros considered a move back to France, which is why Castlemurray stopped featuring in the Bridgestone guides. They have decided to stay put, however, which is great news for food lovers, for M. Delcros is a smashing cook, the views from the dining room of the restaurant are awesomely beautiful, and the rooms are cheap and cosy. This is the prototypical restaurant-with-rooms. (St John's Point, Dunkineely, Tel: (073) 37022, Fax:

37330, castlemurray@eircom.net, Open D, D€, Accommodation rates €€)

A Castlemurray acolyte, Marguerite Howley, cooks excellent food up above the bar in **The Fleet Inn,** a little further west in Killybegs. Lovely fish cookery – though the meat cookery is very fine, also – super desserts, great sounds and great, helpful staff make this a destination address, and if you want to stay there are simple and inexpensive rooms up above the restaurant. (Bridge St, Killybegs, Tel: (073) 31518, Fax: 31664, Open D, D€€)

Close to Donegal is one of the great Irish country houses, Kieran and Amabel Clarke's marvellous **Ardnamona.** The Clarkes are witty, wise people, the house is just darling, and the cooking is excellent: roast red pepper soup; lemon sole with tomato risotto; lamb chops with Puy lentils and colcannon; ricotta and lemon cheesecake. A one night stay isn't enough, believe

South Donegal

us; you should really book at least a couple of nights to get into the spirit of Ardnamona. (Lough Eske, Donegal, Tel: (073) 22650, Fax: 22819, ardnamona.com, info@ardnamona.com, Rates €€)

● There is much simpler accommodation available in Paul Chateanoud's series of cottages, **The Green Gate,** high on the hill just south of Ardara on the N56 up to Dungloe. Some people will find these too austere, for others they represent the true spirit of Donegal, and are a vital discovery. Certainly, breakfast in the garden on a fine summer morning eating Filligan's jams on your toast is hard to beat. Off-beat and off-centre, and thanks for that. (Ardvally, Ardara, Tel: (075) 41546, Rates €)

● The place with the developing reputation in these parts is **Coxtown Manor,** south of Donegal town and two miles from Laghey. Locals love the Belgian waffles they serve with afternoon tea. The foods are well sourced and intelligently cooked, and the house itself is comfortable and pleasing. They even make a good prawn cocktail, for heaven's sake! (Laghey, Tel: (073) 23994, Fax: 23995, mail@coxtownmanor.com, coxtownmanor.com)

THINK LOCAL

The Corncrake takes local ingredients and makes them special...

• **Garden nettles and fresh garden herbs to make a soup**

• **Malin Head crab to pair simply with a vinaigrette**

• **Trawbreaga Bay mussels are crisped with breadcrumbs**

• **Greencastle monkfish is served with a tangy lemon sauce**

• **Wild local salmon is baked in pastry with currants and ginger**

• **Champ is made with local potatoes, flavoured with home-grown lovage**

• **Donegal lamb is served with a rosemary jus**

• **Donegal steak goes with a crème fraîche and local shallots**

• **Garden rhubarb and home-grown blackcurrants are made into ice cream served with ginger biscuits**

Cutting edge cooks

THE HOTTEST PLACES TO EAT IN DUBLIN...

● **Chapter One**

Ross Lewis is a chef on a roll. His restaurant has never been busier, his cooking has never been better, or more enjoyable. And making sure the customer enjoys the food is what he aims for each time; this is flavourful, moreish, mature cooking, and whilst we're not big fans of the room, the service is spot on and value for money is excellent. A brilliant place for dinner both before and after a show in The Gate Theatre.

(Parnell Square, D1. Tel: (01) 873 2266 Fax: 873 2330. Open L&D Tue-Sat. L€€ D€€)

● **The Commons**

Aiden Byrne has revolutionised the cooking in this formal, pretty basement room on St Stephen's Green. This cook is game for any challenge – entire tasting menus centred on tomatoes – and it's a thrill to eat the food of someone as committed to exploring the culinary canon as this young chef. Don't miss the perfect sweetbreads and the superlative salt cod brandade. Hot as it gets.

(Newman House, 85 St Stephen's Gn, D2. Tel: (01) 478 0530 Fax: 478 0551 Open L&D Mon-Fri. L€€ D€€€)

Dublin hotels:

THE CLARENCE

The design of the bedrooms in the Clarence is unmatched in Dublin. We only wish we could say the same about the standard of service, which is a little woozy. But frankly we can forgive them anything after a night in this gorgeous space.

(6-8 Wellington Quay, D2. Tel: (01) 670 9000 Fax: 670 7800 clarence@indigo.ie theclarence.ie Restaurant, rates €€€)

Dublin – The cutting edge cooks

● Cooke's Café

Johnny Cooke's café is many people's favourite place to eat in the city, with deliciously delectable cooking from the boss and a great room in which to linger. Many changes are due to take place early in 2002, with the opening of a more informal restaurant, selling gourmet pizzas, oysters and brasserie food. Given its pedigree, we expect the restaurant (and watch out for a possible name change) to remain one of the key destinations in the city, nothing less, with the coolest crowd you can find.

(14 Sth William St, D2, Tel: (01) 679 0536/7/8 Fax: 679 0546 cookes1@iol.ie cookescafe.com Open all day Mon-Sun. Meals €€)

● L'Ecrivain

Derry and Sally-Anne Clarke run the best room in the city, a handsome, loveable space with great service where Mr Clarke and his team produce some of the finest modern Irish food you can eat: roast stuffed saddle of rabbit with a Paris brown mushroom sauce retains pure flavours whilst giving a toothy rusticity; their home-cured mackerel is benchmark; dishes such as oysters with a Guinness sabayon are purest magic. This unmissable destination is the capital's hottest spot.

(109 Lwr Baggot St, D2, Tel: (01) 661 1919 Fax: 661 0617 enquiries@lecrivain.com lecrivain.com Open L Mon-Fri, & D Mon-Sat. L€€, D€€€€)

Dublin Hotels:

THE CLARION

The office-style chic of the Clarion is appropriate for its position, slap bang in Dublin's financial district. The ethos of this hotel is sanctity for stressed out financiers, with its muted colours and minimalist design ethic. The Sinergie restaurant has yet to find true synergy. (International Financial Services Centre, D1, Tel: (01) 433 8800 Fax: 433 8811 clarionhotelifsc.com Restaurant & Bar, Rates €€€)

The cutting edge cooks – Dublin

● Halo @ The Morrison

Not as clamorous now as when the dotcommers were on a roll, but Jean Michel Poulot's fusion cooking is superb – nobody does it better – and the dining room is vividly dramatic and glamorous, which makes Halo a great date restaurant. The food is very exciting: scallops served with yams seasoned with Sichuan pepper; monkfish with saffron mash; Japanese pepper ice cream. And then, downstairs to Lobo, after dinner, for dancing and wild drinks until the wee small hours with all the urgent hipsters.

(Morrison Hotel, Ormond Quay, D1. Tel: (01) 887 2400 Fax: 874 4039 info@morrisonhotel.ie morrisonhotel.ie. Open L&D Mon-Sun. L€€, D€€€)

● Jacob's Ladder

Adrian Roche's simple, upstairs dining room is as subtle and singular as this fine chef's lovely cooking. Restraint, maturity and an utterly true instinct for combining flavours makes for some of the city's most enjoyable and innovative cooking: the shellfish coddle is a Dublin city classic; the potato soup with pea and truffle ravioli is demon; the vegetarian dishes, such as courgettes with peppers and walnuts and a gratin of haricot beans with wild mushroom fumé, show true respect for vegetarians. Indeed, respect for the customer is the gift of this fine restaurant.

(4/5 Nassau Street, D2 Tel: (01) 670 3865 Fax: 670 3868. Open L Tue-Fri, D Tue-Sat. L€€ D€€)

Dublin Hotels:

THE HIBERNIAN

A very discreet location off Lower Baggot Street makes this a great hideaway haven, beloved by its many regulars and superbly run by great staff managed by David Butt. It's the service that will bring you back into this quietly comfortable space.

Eastmoreland Place, (Ballsbridge, D4, Tel: (01) 668 7666 Fax: 660 2655 info@hibernianhotel.com slh.com/hibernia Restaurant Room rates: €€€)

Dublin – The cutting edge cooks

● The Mermaid Café

Ben Gorman's cooking is quite unlike anyone else's. Technique seems relatively unimportant to him, so his food is simply presented, and focuses all the time on capturing integral flavours and implicit textures. There is nowhere else in the city quite like it, and the ambience and the cool sounds make the Mermaid some sort of bohemian heaven.

Benchmark dishes include the New England crab cakes; the Atlantic seafood casserole; the veal sweetbreads with saffron and jasmine rice. Ultra cool.
(69-70 Dame St, Temple Bar, D2, Tel: (01) 670 8236 Fax: 670 8205 mermaid@iol.ie mermaid.ie Open L&D Mon-Sun (brunch Sun & hols) B€, L€€, D€€)

cool

● One Pico

One Pico has moved to what was, once upon a time, Polo One, and Eamonn O'Reilly's singular, complex and artfully contrived food finally has the sort of swish room it always needed in the right part of town.

The cooking can trip itself up with complexity, but at full tilt it offers something with a touch of magic, and the combinations here can show true originality: tarte tatin of caramelised onion and goat's cheese; a cep and sage cream with chicken; red wine fumé with roast spiced salmon; fantastic baked chevre cheesecake.
(Schoolhouse Lane, D2, Tel: (01) 676 0300, onepico.com Open L&D L€€, D€€€)

funky

Dublin Hotels:

THE MORGAN

Even with the noise of revellers on Fleet Street – and they can be very noisy – for us this is the great city-centre romantic hideaway, a style-lover's paradise. The larger suites are the ones to go for if you can afford them. Hopefully new ownership will sort out the Bar and the Café.
10 Fleet St, D2. Tel: (01) 679 3939 Fax: 679 3946 sales@themorgan.com themorgan.com Rates €€€)

The cutting edge cooks – Dublin

The Tea Room

The merit of Antony Ely's cooking is shown by the fact that loads of other chefs come to the Clarence Hotel to eat his food, and yet this is not cheffy food: Ely's cooking is grounded in true flavours, and he loves simple things, like rump of lamb with cocotte potatoes, and cod with champ, and well-made ice creams. True, he brings quite a polish to the presentation, but this is truly comfort food, beautifully accomplished. Lovely room, but service has been inconsistent recently.
(The Clarence Hotel, 6-8 Wellington Quay, D2.
Tel: (01) 670 9000 Fax: 670 7800 clarence@indigo.ie theclarence.ie Open lunch & dinner (brunch on Sun) L€€, D€€€)

Thornton's

Kevin and Muriel Thornton's restaurant is a classically comfortable room overlooking the canal at Portobello, with food that is stratospheric in its ambition and execution. Everything seems as if it is improvised, yet the wealth of detail in dishes such as the extraordinary roasted scallops with braised white onions and white truffle are breathtaking. High prices, yet superb value for money given the quality of ingredients this chef insists on using. Inspirational cooking which simply cannot be missed.
(1 Portobello Road, D8.
Tel: (01) 454 9067 Fax: 453 2947. thorntons@iol.ie. Open Lunch on Fri, Dinner Tue-Sat. Lunch €€€, Dinner €€€)

Dublin Hotels:

THE MORRISON

Give us a front-of-house room overlooking the River Liffey and the Millennium bridge and, like most everyone else, you will have to physically drag us away from the hyper-stylish Morrison.
As swish as it gets, design by John Rocha.
(Lwr Ormond Quay, D1 Tel: (01) 887 2400 Fax: (01) 874 4039 info@morrisonhotel.ie morrisonhotel.ie Restaurant (see Halo @ The Morrison) Room rates from €€€)

Ethnic Dublin

CHINESE

● The best ethnic cooking in Dublin has to be hunted down. For something close to authentic Chinese food, then you have to go to **The China-Sichuan** in Kilmacud, to the most unprepossessing location imaginable for a good restaurant – it's smack in the middle of a row of shops in a suburban wasteland. No matter; the food is good – black sole with scallions; super tofu with black bean sauce; bak choi with garlic sauce – and everyone loves it, so if you are planning a family Sunday lunch, then book well in advance.
(4 Lower Kilmacud Rd, Stillorgan, Co Dublin, Tel: (01) 288 4817 Fax: 288 0882. Open L&D Mon-Sun. L€€, D€€)

● **The Furama,** opposite the rugby ground in Donnybrook, is another long-established Chinese restaurant which makes a minimum of compromises. Good, energising cooking – roast Duck Cantonese; fine prawns with black bean sauce; salt and pepper squid. The Furama is also a great date restaurant: discreet, sophisticated and mannerly. (88 Donnybrook Rd, D4, Tel: (01) 283 0522. Open L&D Mon-Sun. L€€, D€€)

● Then take a walk on the wild side; dim sum in the city at the weekends is where to get the real thing. Try **The Good World** on Gt George's Street for cutting edge dim sum (you know it's real because on Sunday morning everyone else here is Chinese) and another popular spot is the **Imperial Chinese Restaurant** on Wicklow Street. The mainstream food here is standard, but the dim sum is glutinous, gloopy, fiddly and fun, and it's great value. (Good World, 18 Sth Gt George's St, D2, Tel: (01) 677 5373) (Imperial, 12a Wicklow Street, D2, Tel: (01) 677 2580 Both open L&D. L€, D€€)

Ethnic Dublin

INDIAN

● For us, the best Indian food in Dublin comes out of a small little café stuck at the edge of a dull shopping centre in dull old Glenageary. **The Bombay Pantry** is a take-away with a few little tables run by Vivek Sahni and it can really come up with the goods, producing food that is deftly and sensitively seasoned and uncompromised. A second branch in Rathmines has now opened. (Glenageary Shopping Centre. Tel: (01) 285 6683. 14 Rathgar Road, Rathmines, Tel: (01) 496 9695. Open L&D. Meals €)

● In the city itself, **Jaipur,** on the corner of Stephen St and Sth George's St is regarded by many as the most exciting Indian cooking in town, but we find their experiments sometimes self-conscious rather than inspired, though we applaud their attempt to move away from the balti-tandoori cliché.
(Sth Gt George's St, Tel: (01) 677 0999 Fax: 677 0979. Open D. D€€)

● For something interesting with Indian food, then head to the **Poppadum** restaurant in Rathgar, just at the traffic junction at the church. The design here is deliberately non-ethnic, and the food pushes at the boundaries of what we expect from Indian food with considerable success.
(91 Rathgar Rd, D6 Tel: (01) 490 2383. Open D. D€€)

PACIFIC RIM

● **AYA** on Clarendon Street has been the runaway success story for ethnic foods in Dublin recently, with new branches opening in the IFSC and in Donnybrook. Purists quibble about authenticity, but AYA is really a fun theme on Japanese food rather than something echt, and it's none the worse for that. You can get everything from conveyor-belt sushi to an Irish breakfast at the weekends, all done with great style and great service.

Ethnic Dublin

Teenagers love it. (rere Brown Thomas, Clarendon Street, D2 Tel: (01) 677 1544 mail@aya.ie. aya.ie. Open L&D. Meals €-€€)

● **Bangkok Cafe** attracted the attention of a very hip, smart set, who loved the frisson of its inner city location and its nouveau pauvre style and street food grub. Inconsistencies, however, have crept in as success increased. We hope they can reconcile these tensions, because on song, it's a real fun place. Just don't wear your glad rags. (106 Parnell St, D1, Tel: (01) 878 6618, Open D, D€€)

● We love the design and the lighting in **Wagamama,** at the St Stephen's Green shopping centre, and the noodles here are a lot better than the ones in the London branches. It's a good spot to grab something fast before going to the movies or a gig. (Sth King St, D2. Tel: (01) 478 2152. Open L&D. Meals €-€€)

● **Yamamori Noodles** on South Great George's Street has more relaxed service, and the cooking can be very enjoyable, but the design is a little too much in the bricolage style for us. (71 Sth Gt George's St, D2 Tel: (01) 475 5001. Open L&D. Meals €-€€)

AYA'S TOP SELLING SUSHI

■ **SALMON NIGIRI**
Salmon, vinegared rice

■ **EBI TEMPURA-MAKI**
Prawn Tempura

■ **PRAWN NIGIRI**
Prawn, vinegared rice

■ **CALIFORNIA MAKI**
Crab stick, avocado

■ **SHIMESABA SASHIMI**
Mackerel marinated in rice vinegar and salted

■ **TUNA NIGIRI**
Tuna, vinegared rice.

■ **TUNA SASHIMI**
Raw tuna with dipping sauce and wasabi

■ **SALMON SASHIMI**
Raw salmon with dipping sauce and wasabi

■ **UNAGI-NIGIRI**
Grilled Conger Eel

■ **KAPPA-MAKI**
Cucumber & sesame

Big night

PLACES TO DRESS AND IMPRESS...

● Restaurant Patrick Guilbaud

The sheer polish of RPG means it is a most impressive place to bring someone for a first visit, and the service is as consummate as it gets. It is hard to beat for business entertaining thanks to that service, but a business clientele can tend to dominate the ambience of the room.
(21 Upr Merrion St, D2
Tel: (01) 676 4192. Open L&D.
L€€€, D€€€)

● Peacock Alley

Conrad Gallagher opened in London's Shaftesbury Avenue in summer 2001, to good reviews, but his plans are to relaunch and devote future time to the original Peacock Alley. Full-on flavour food is the order of the day in a beautiful room, with tall constructions and challenging flavours, and with Gallagher at the stove it can be as sublime as it is expensive. (The Fitzwilliam Hotel, St Stephen's Green, D2. Tel: (01) 662 0760. Open L&D. L€€, D€€)

● Roly's Bistro

Visitors to Dublin often book dinner in Roly's even before they book a hotel room,

and the thunderous atmosphere of Colin O'Daly's restaurant explains why this icon address remains such a success. Paul Cartwright's food is smashing – quintessential brasserie cooking with expert execution – the crowd are always having the time of their life, and so are you. Roly's is part of the fabric of the city.
(7 Ballsbridge Terrace, Ballsbridge, D4 Tel: (01) 668 2611 Fax: 660 8535. Open L&D. L€€, D€€€)

Big Night Dublin

● Shanahan's on the Green
John Shanahan's big, brassy restaurant is really an American steak house, but done with admirable over-the-top grandeur and verve. Superb meat cookery, brilliant service, great sounds (classic crooners at high volume), high prices and, it seems, the destination address for every American visiting Dublin. (119 St Stephen's Gr, D2, Tel: (01) 407 0939 Fax: 407 0940. Open D. D€€€)

TEMPLE BAR

Temple Bar has loads of restaurants, and most of them can be safely ignored. These you need to know:

• The Tea Room,
where Anthony Ely is really making his mark with some outstanding cooking, making this a true cutting-edge space. (Tel: (01) 670 9000. Open L&D. €€€)

• The Mermaid Café
on Dame Street (with its funky sister restaurant **Gruel**) is one of the city's great addresses and produces true, original and mega-tasty cooking and awesome Bloody Marys! (Tel: (01) 670 8236 Open L&D €€)

• The brilliant **Dish** on Crow Street, has the coolest sounds and superb food and, with The Mermaid, is one of the great weekend brunch destinations. (Tel: (01) 671 1248. Open L&D €€)

• Bar Italia, at the edge of Temple Bar, where you get real Italian cooking from Stefano Crescenzi and – Vital! Vital! – what may be the finest espresso in the city. Don't miss this. (Tel: (01) 679 5128 Open L. €)

• Another address city dwellers use is **Il Baccaro,** a little basement wine bar at the corner of Meetinghouse Square, which provides some of the best fun to be had in the capital – just don't drink too much of that interestingly rustic wine they serve. Is it really 3am already? (Tel: (01) 671 4597. Open nights. €€)

• The stylish **Eden,** which has passed through its fashionable phase to become a good, grown-up restaurant, is a great place, and also serves some of the very best cocktails in the city. (Tel: (01) 670 5372. Open L&D €€)

• The Chameleon is a nice, simple and genuine restaurant with a distinctive style of Indonesian food. (Tel: (01) 671 0362 Open D €€)

• The **Elephant & Castle** has recently had a change of management, but the old reliable dishes are as reliable as ever. (Tel: (01) 679 3121 Open all day. €€)

• For reliable, old-fashioned-and-thanks-for-that French cookery, then **Les Freres Jacques** is a discreet and enjoyable restaurant, albeit somewhat expensive. (Tel: (01) 679 4555. Open L&D €€€)

Dubliner's delights

CULT ADDRESSES IN THE CITY CENTRE...

● **Avoca Handweavers**
Join the queue snaking down the stairs in this smart shop, and wait patiently to enjoy some of the nicest,  truest cooking in town. Avoca has other great food branches in Wicklow, but the Dublin store is a must visit, and don't forget to buy their wonderful book of recipes. Nice food-to-go in the shop in the basement.
(Suffolk St, D2, Tel: (01) 677 4215. info@avoca.ie. avoca.ie. Open day-time Mon-Sun. L€)

● **Bond**
Karl Purdy and his team run a happening place in Beresford Place, across from the IFSC, which has been best described as a "wine shop with waiters", i.e. there is a wine bar/shop downstairs where you select your bottle, then head back upstairs for lunch (if you can get a table) or dinner. The wines are very keenly priced, and you drink them here for a great deal less than most restaurants. (5 Beresford Place, D1, Tel: (01) 855 9244. Open L & D. L€, D€€)

● **Bruno's** has become a real food lover's favourite in the city centre, thanks to mature cooking that eschews any culinary grandstanding, and focusses instead on delivering solid and true flavours.
(21 Kildare St, Tel: (01) 662 4724, brunos.ie, Open L&D, L€€, D€€€€)

● **Café Mao** is another expanding chain, with a second branch in Dun Laoghaire at the pavilion as well as the original on Chatham Street.
What they do is basically Asia's Greatest Culinary Hits, with a melting pot of dishes culled from the Pacific Rim

Dublin City Centre

countries and these are fun, laid-back places to hang out.
2/3 Chatham Row, D2 Tel: (01) 670 4899. Fax: 670 4999. The Pavilion, Dun Laoghaire Seafront, Tel: (01) 214 8090 cafemao.com. Open L&D. Meals €€.

● **Cavistons Fish Bar** The centre city outpost of the Glasthule fishy phenomenon, is one of the cult addresses in the city. Spankingly fresh fish, simply prepared; get ready to be addicted. (Epicurean Food Mall, Middle Abbey St, D1 Tel: (01) 878 2289. Open daily. L€)

● **Cornucopia** The Dublin vegetarian's first choice, it seems, now and always. Old style, for sure, but always enjoyable. (19 Wicklow St, D2, Tel: (01) 677 7583. Open L & early D. Meals €-€€)

● **Dish** One of the great city restaurants. Understated, utterly un-selfconscious, it is home to great modern Irish cooking, the finest collection of sounds you can hear anywhere, and it has a

nobility and charm which belie its modest room.
(2 Crow St, D2 Tel: (01) 671 1248 Fax: 671 1249 dishrestaurant.net dish@indigo.ie. Open L&D. Lunch €, Dinner €€)

● **Dobbin's Wine Bistro**
It's been here since before the flood, it's got simple food, gingham tablecloths, sawdust on the floor and millionaires spending serious money packed into its booths. Lunch in Dobbin's is a rite of passage in Dublin business life. Cancel the afternoon. (15 Stephen's Lane, D2, Tel: (01) 661 3321 dobbinswinebistro@eircom.net Open L&D, L€€, D€€)

● **Dunne & Crescenzi**
Italian cheese and salamis, with a glass of wine, is for many Dubliners one of the great city secrets in Eileen Crescenzi's beautiful shop cum café. Get there early at lunchtime or you will have to wait whilst everyone else is scoffing.
(14 Sth Frederick St, D2 Tel: (01) 677 3815. Fax: 677 3815. Open Daily. L€)

● Ely

Erik Robson runs Dublin's cult wine bar, just off
Merrion Row, which has a magnificent wine list with
loads of good wines available by the glass, and
some excellent food: don't miss the organic meat
from the family farm in County Clare. A brilliant spot.
(22 Ely Place, D2 Tel: (01) 676 8986. Open L&D. Meals €€)

● The Expresso Bar and Café

The original Expresso remains a happy haunt in leafy
Ballsbridge, whilst the new outlet in the IFSC is a
lifesaver for health conscious bankers who enjoy the
light and well judged modern cooking. Chargrilled
tuna, Penne with smoked chicken.
(St Mary's Rd, Tel: (01) 660 0585, Open daily, L€, D€) (The
IFSC, Dublin Tel: 672 1812, Open L, L€)

● The Gotham Café

The Gotham is one of the cult addresses for
teenagers, and for parents with wannabe
adolescents, thanks to the good, properly made
pizzas and other snappy foods, and the enjoyably
retro décor: Let's hope you're not old enough to
remember when those Rolling Stone covers were first published.
(5 Sth Anne St, D2. Tel: (01) 679 5266. Open L&D. Meals €-€€)

● Gruel

Ben Gorman serves what he himself sums up as 'short order cooking,
but nice'. A soup kitchen cum restaurant he serves three or four
soups with food such as smoked haddock fish cakes, half roast
chickens, tortillas and loads of salads. They also serve 'food to go'
which they market as gourmet TV dinners, and they have recently
started serving brunch. Soup, then, and go next door to the Mermaid
for the nuts, their spicy pecans are ace. (67 Dame Street, D2. Tel: (01)
670 7119. Open daily Mon-Sun. Meals €-€€)

Dublin City Centre

● **Itsabagel**
Every hip office worker in Dublin seems to get their lunch in Itsabagel. Real bagels, chic fillings, cool website.
(Epicureal Mall D1 Tel: (01) 874 0486, itsabagel.com, Open daily, L€)

● **Kevin Arundel @ Number Ten** Another basement restaurant in the business sector, in Longfields Hotel, and Kevin Arundel is knockin' 'em dead with good cooking – duck leg with polenta; monkfish with carrot and ginger consommé; salmon with fennel à la grecque – and great value for money.
(9-10 Fitzwilliam St Lwr, D2, Tel: (01) 676 136, Open L&D, L€, D€€)

● **Moe's** John Connelly has made a great success with his flavourful, well-judged modern Irish cooking in this little basement room at the junction of Fitzwilliam Street and Baggot Street. Very good value lunches, which are a feature of the restaurants in this business belt.
(112 Lr Baggot St, D2. Tel: (01) 676 7610. Fax: (01) 676 7610. moesdublin@hotmail.com moesdublin.com. Open L&D. L€€, D€€)

● **Ocean** Ocean has had a brief and interesting life so far, but under the control of Andy Neiland it is beginning to get a reputation for some fine cooking.
(Charlotte Quay Dock, Ringsend, D1, Tel: (01) 668 8862, Open L&D, L€, D€€)

● **101 Talbot** If a centre city restaurant can be described as having a neighbourhood style, then 101 is it. Brilliant service from Paschal Bradley and some of the most sensible, unpretentious and delicious cooking – especially their vegetarian cooking - to be found in Dublin, at decent prices. Priceless, nothing less, and great for youngsters and teenagers.
(100-102 Talbot St, D1, Tel: (01) 874 5011 Fax: 874 5011. pascalbradley@tinet.ie. Open D. D€€)

● **Pearl Brasserie** Sebastian Masi used to cook complex food in The Commons, down the road

Dublin City Centre

on St Stephen's Green, but seems more at home with the brasserie cooking he is offering in the Pearl: duck magret with quenelles of goat's cheese; roast monkfish in bacon, nice lunch food such as croque monsieur and steak with sauté potatoes. (20 Merrion St, Uppr, Tel: (01) 661 3627, Open L & D, L€, D€€)

● **Queen of Tarts** Regina and Yvonne Fallon run the best-loved café in the city, and for those who can't get in to the Dame St branch, a new outpost has opened in the City Hall Café. Fab meringues, crumbles, muffins, super sandwiches and tarts pull in the crowds. (Cork Hill, D2, Tel: (01) 670 7499. Open daily. L€)

● **Soup Dragon**
This is proof that Capel Street is beginning to happen, Soup Dragon is a funky place with bar stools, serving mostly soups from a blackboard menu. Cool crockery and nice cooking; check out the Thai chicken soup and the haddock chowder. (168 Capel St, D1, Tel: (01) 872 3277, Open L, L€)

● **The Trocadero**
Nope, the 'Troc doesn't do retro design; it's always been like this. It ain't broke, so they don't fix it. Steak, chips, and lots of wine, and is that the time already? Pure cult. (3 St Andrew's St, D2, Tel: (01) 677 5545. Open D. D€€)

Little Italy:

• Steps of Rome on Chatham St is the most cultish Italian place in town. The strangest and best slices of pizza you can find in Dublin. (Chatham St, D2 Tel: (01) 670 5630. Open L&D. Meals €)

• The same owners run Ar Vicioletto on Crow St, in Temple Bar which has some nice simple food. (5 Crow St, Temple Bar, Tel: (01) 670 8662, Open L&D, L€, D€€)

• Do check out Botticelli in Temple Bar. It can be inconsistent, but also can be the best for cuccina casalinga. (3 Temple Bar, D2, Tel: (01) 672 7289 Open L&D, L€, D€, €€€)

• Nicos (53 Dame St, Tel: (01) 677 3062, Open L&D, L€€, D€€€) is the original of the species and Da Pino is friendly and fun. (38 Parliament St, Tel: (01) 671 9308, Open L&D, L€, D€€)

South Dublin

Neighbourhood places

SOUTHSIDE

• •

RANELAGH & RATHMINES

Tribeca is the hot spot in Ranelagh, so much so that folk even queue in the rain to get in for Sunday brunch. The benchmark spicy chicken wings pull them in, but the organic burgers are also great, the lemonade is ace, the sounds are cool. A great 'hood restaurant. (Tribeca, 65 Ranelagh, D6, Tel: (01) 497 4174. Open L&D. L€, D€€) Just down the Ranelagh strip, **Nectar** is great for wraps, juices and smoothies, and has extended to a second branch in the city on Exchequer Street.

(Nectar Juice Bar, 53 Ranelagh Village, D6, Tel: (01) 491 0934. Exchequer St Tel: (01) 672 7501. Open L&D. L€, D€)
The other neighbourhood hits are **Dunville Place**, on Dunville Avenue, which has a big local following for Mick Duignan's smart and very flavourful modern Irish cooking (Dunville Avenue, Ranelagh, D6, Tel: (01) 496 8181. Open L&D. L€, D€€) and also the extra-friendly, family-run **Crema,** in the centre of Rathmines, which is a pure delight of a place with lovely dessert baking, great vegetarian food and, especially, don't-miss-'em soups.
(312 Lwr Rathmines Rd, D6 Tel: (01) 496 5555. Open L, L€)

BALLSBRIDGE

The Lobster Pot: The 'Pot hasn't changed in decades, and it doesn't need to: creamy, lush, pricey seafood cookery, a cosy upstairs room and great, old-style, proper service that simply never dates. A true treat, whatever age you are. (9 Ballsbridge Tce, D4, Tel: (01) 660 9170, Fax: 668 0025. Open L&D, L€€€, D€€€)

South Dublin

O'Connells, a smart room in the basement of the Bewley's Aparthotel is a shrine for food lovers, as well as a favourite haunt for prosperous southsiders. Lovely cooking by Brian McCarthy, based on diligently sourced Irish ingredients, and make sure to try the grills from their wood-burning stove, which are exceptional, especially the exquisite duck.
(Bewley's Aparthotel, Merrion Rd, Ballsbridge, D4, Tel: (01) 647 3304, Fax: 647 3499. oconnellsballsbridge@eircom.net, oconnellsballsbridge.com, Open L&D, L€, D€€)

In **Seasons @ Four Seasons Hotel** Terry White's cooking is poised, restrained and confident, based on superb ingredients and, best of all, focused on a lightness and delicacy that makes it a pleasure to eat. But more assurance is needed in the service to pull all the elements of this huge operation together.
Make sure to tour the hotel, ignoring the overblown decor, in order to check out the glorious and effervescent flower arrangements.
(Four Seasons Hotel, Simmonscourt Rd, Ballsbridge, D4, Tel: (01) 655 4000, Fax: 665 4099, fourseasons.com, Open B, L&D. B€€€, L€€€, D€€€).

BLACKROCK
The Blackrock Bistro. Old-timers may still call it Blueberries, but TBB has carved out its own identity as the destination address in downtown Blackrock, thanks to smart cooking and service from Ryan Oudjadi and Eric Marechal. Don't miss the brioche pain perdu, with chocolate mousse and caramel sauce: it's a stunner. Very good value for your money. (above Jack O'Rourke's pub, 15 Main Street, Blackrock, Co Dublin, Tel: (01) 278 8900, Open L&D L€, D€€)
Dali's is a very popular dining room with locals, with cautiously flavoured modern cooking.
(63/65 Main St, Blackrock, Co Dublin, Tel: (01) 278 0660, Fax: 278 0661, Open L&D, L€, D€€€)

South Dublin

CABINTEELY

Rodney's Bistro is a nice little place, very much a local place for local folk who value its consistency. The food is modern - but not too modern – and is spirited and fun.
(Cabinteely Village, Tel: (01) 285 1664. Open D, D€-€€)

DALKEY

After an uncertain start, **Kish** has begun to find its signature, and it's a serious, rather expensive, special occasion signature at that. It's a gorgeous room, with beautiful views over Dalkey bay, and for a treat it's an excellent big-night-out sort of place with bourgeois cooking. (Coliemore Rd, Dalkey, Co Dublin, Tel: (01) 285 0377, Fax: (01) 285 0141, Open L&D, L€€, *D€€€)*

The food is very, very simple in **Nosh** – fish and chips, bangers and mash, Caesar salad – but the slickness of the delivery of the dishes and the swish room has made it a whiz-bang success. The bowls for the Caesar salad are too deep, but it doesn't stop everyone from going back. (111 Coliemore Rd, Dalkey, Co Dublin, Tel: (01) 284 0666, nosh.ie, Open L&D, L€, D€€)

Idlewild in Patrick Street is where locals go for good breakfasts and good lunches at decent prices, and they will be opening the restaurant for dinner from autumn 2001 (after we go to press). (20 Patrick St, Dalkey, Co Dublin, Tel: (01) 235 4501, Open B&L, B€, *L€)*

The Queens pub has long been a local favourite in Dalkey, where as well as bar food, their more formal restaurant, **Vico** specialises in char grills. (The Queens, 12 Castle St, Dalkey, Co Dublin, Tel: (01) 285 4569, Fax: 285 8345, queens@clubi.ie. Open D, D€€)

For many folk, the Thai cooking in Tony Ecock's **Thai House** restaurant is the best to be found in Dublin, and the Thai House is always a good, special occasion, big-night-out destination. (21 Railway Rd, Dalkey, Tel: (01) 284 7304. Open Dinner, D€€)

FOXROCK

Bistro One Mark Shannon's clubby upstairs room is a true southside success story. Packed with locals who enjoy the comfort food and the comfortable ambience. (Foxrock Village, D18, Tel: (01) 289 7711, Fax: 289 9858, Open D, D€€)

GLASTHULE

Caviston's may be the best-loved restaurant in the entire city, perhaps even the entire country. The great fish cookery from chef Noel Cusack, so adroit and simple, so well-judged, the brilliant atmosphere created by superb staff and the burble of the happiest customers on the southside, mean that the only problem is getting a table. Unmissable. (59 Glasthule Rd, Dun Laoghaire, Co Dublin, Tel: (01) 280 9245, Fax: 284 4054, caviston@indigo.ie, cavistons.com, Open three lunch sittings, L€€)

Dunne & Couzy's superb first-floor restaurant, **Duzys,** has been one of the most consistent and creative on the southside for several years now, and the recent improvements to the room make it even better. Great cooking by John Dunne pays respect to bistro tradition: green beans with fillet; onion soup; pecan pie; superb duck confit. Apart from playing Madonna CDs, they don't put a foot wrong.

(18 Glasthule Road, Dun Laoghaire, Co Dublin, Tel: (01) 230 0210, Fax: 230 0466, duzyscafe@clubi.ie, Open L&D, L€-€€, D€€)

SANDYMOUNT

Browne's Delicatessen offers the clever formula of filled ciabattas to eat in or take out, plus the succulent savoury baking from Sarah Webb's Gallic Kitchen. Home made soups, sandwiches and good coffee make this address the best in the immediate area.

(18 Sandymount Green Tel: (01) 269 7316. Open L, L€)

Essential statistics:

Budget to open a Four Seasons Hotel in Dublin?
The official figure is 'in excess of £65million'. The unofficial figure goes up in tens of millions, depending on which taxi driver you are speaking to.

North Dublin

NORTHSIDE

RAHENY

Il Fornaio is a cult address for handmade pizzas, which you can eat in or take away. There are pastas, salads and bruschetta also, but it is the pizzas which are the object of your desire and which pull in foodlovers for miles around.
(55 Kilbarrack Rd, Raheny, D5, Tel: 1890 482542, Open daily, €)

HOWTH

Aqua This lovely room took some time to find its direction, but Charlie Smith's restaurant is on a roll right now, with assured, smart food you always crave: scallop salad with mango and chilli; grilled asparagus with balsamic and Parmesan; dry-aged sirloin with roast potatoes. (1 West Pier, Howth, Tel: (01) 832 0690, Open L&D, L€, D€€)

The King Sitric Smart new rooms have made the venerable Sitric an even better destination, and the lovely new dining room is home to some spirited and imaginative fish cookery from chef-boss Aidan McManus. (East Pier, Howth, Co Dublin, Tel: (01) 832 5235, Fax: 839 2442, info@kingsitric.ie, kingsitric.com, Open L&D, L€€, D€€€)

MALAHIDE

There are some fine talented culinary veterans cooking as well as ever on the northside, and, in **Bon Appetit,** Patsy McGuirk is one of the best. Classical food, serene ambience, good service, and happy customers. These veterans make it seem easy, don't they?
(9 James Tce, Malahide, Co Dublin, Tel: (01) 845 0314, Fax: 845 0314, info@bonappetit.ie, bonappetit.ie, Open L&D, L€€, *D€€€)*

The Chuck Wagon:

The sweetest culinary secret for folks heading North out of Dublin is just at the edge of the road as you leave Swords behind. The Chuck Wagon roadside caravan, is where everyone pulls over for the sausage and bacon soda bread sarnies.

SKERRIES

As with Howth's King Sitric, adding excellent new rooms has made Terry McCoy's **The Red Bank Guesthouse & Restaurant** an even better destination for dinner and an overnight stay. The chef does some mighty impressive fish cookery, and the old style of the dining room is a delight. (6 & 7 Church St, Skerries, Co Dublin, Tel: (01) 849 1005, Fax: 849 1598, redbank@eircom.net, redbank.ie, Open D & Sun L, L€€, D€€€)

SMITHFIELD

It's all getting a little bit posh in the Smithfield-Stoneybatter quarter these days, so thank heavens for the true market man's café which is **Paddy's Place.** If you seek a dish of Dublin coddle, you will find it here, along with bacon sarnies, mugs of tea and lots of other good kick-start, early-start food. (Corporation Mkt, D7, Tel: (01) 873 5130. Open 6am-2.30pm (from 7am-11am Sat). L€)

STONEYBATTER

Gus and Teresa Hernandez's smashing new **Mero Mero Café,** on Manor Street, is another sign of the trading-up of dear old Stoneybatter. Come here for true, authentic Mexican cooking, the like of which is as rare as hen's teeth in these islands. (56A Manor Street, Stoneybatter, D7, Tel: (01) 670 7799, sabormex@indigo.ie, open daily, L€)

Then & now

THE KING SITRIC

'When we first opened we had six main dishes of meat, to one main dish of fish (plaice); now we have twelve mains of fish, and one meat.'

THE RED BANK

'People always wanted chips: fish and chips, or steak and chips. Now they want locally caught fish and potato cakes, skins, or gratin. Anything but chips!'

BON APPETIT

'When we opened the most popular dish was Pork Maurice, escalope of pork stuffed with cheese and ham. Now the favourite would be - Creation Sole McGuirk - sole grilled on the bone, filled with turbot & prawns.'

Brunch bunch

BRUNCH IS BIG IN DUBLIN...

THE MERMAID CAFÉ

The best Bloody Marys, incredible vodka-laced watermelon, sublime cooking, and if you have a truly bad hangover they will even give you extra homefries to get you through that green-around-the-gills phase.

DISH

We'll have the wonderful French toast with maple, the benchmark eggs Florentine, the cool white wine and the zingy coffee one more time, please, Gerard, but could you kindly turn down the Supertramp CD?

ODESSA

This is where you and your mates hang out with your hangovers: spend two or three hours in Odessa, slumped in a comfy sofa, with pitchers of Bloody Mary, and soon the world will start to seem logical again. The food is fine.

TRIBECA

If you are a late riser, you will have to join the queue and wait to get your mushroom and herb omelette and mug of coffee and cool lemonade. Never mind. Talk about Marshall MacLuhan in a loud voice and annoy someone.

NOSH

The Farrell sisters' smart room on Coliemore Road is very popular with young Dalkey folk who crave the simple comfort food laced with zippy, fatty succulence they specialise in. Porridge with syrup, bacon and black pudding cake, full-on weekend fry-up.

EXPRESSO BAR

I'll share a taste of my bubble & squeak so long as I can have a taste of your smoked fish cakes, how does that sound to you? You don't want to share? Do we need to talk about what we mean to each other after all this time?

Georgian Dublin

GREAT TOWNHOUSES...

● Browne's

Location, location, location! You have always wanted to stay on St Stephen's Green, and Browne's is the place to do it. Very well run by a good team under Justin Greene, and with good food in the brasserie. (22 St Stephen's Green, D2, Tel: (01) 638 3939. Fax: 638 3900, info@brownesdublin.com, brownesdublin.com, Open L&D, L€€, D€€, Room rates €€€)

● No 31

The ultimate cult address in the city; check out the magnificent retro-style sitting room. (31 Leeson Close, D2, Tel: (01) 676 5011, Fax: 676 2929, number31@iol.ie, number31.ie. Room €€€)

● Fitzwilliam Park Hotel

Not to be confused with the St Stephen's Green Fitzwilliam, this is a discreet, Georgian town house hotel, the views from the front, out across Dublin are amazing. (5 Fitzwilliam Sq, D2 Tel: (01) 662 8280 Fax: 662 8281 fitzpark.ie, info@fitzpark.ie, Rates €€€)

● Anglesea House

OK, not Georgian – but a nice old Victorian house in leafy Ballsbridge, and home to the most gargantuan breakfast in the city: allow at least 90 minutes for breakfast, seriously! (63 Anglesea Rd, Ballsbridge, D4, Tel: (01) 668 3877, Fax: 668 3461. Rate €€)

● Simmonstown House

OK. OK! Again not Georgian, but a beautiful town house, just across from the RDS in Ballsbridge, which is magnificently run and offers wonderful cooking at breakfast. (Sydenham Rd, Ballsbridge, D4, Tel: (01) 660 7260, Fax: 660 7341 simmonstownhouse.com, Rate €€)

● Waterloo House

Great location, good value and nice breakfasts explain the steady success of the fine Waterloo House. (Waterloo Rd, D4, Tel: (01) 660 1888, Fax: 667 1955, waterloohouse.ie Rate €€)

Galway: where to eat

● The smart locals parcel up their eating like this: for fun funky food in a whacky, libertine ambience, they go down to the Spanish Arch to **Nimmo's,** where Harriet Leander and her team produce some neat cooking: good fish soup; nice beef bourguignonne, good vegetarian dishes such as aubergine bake; excellent desserts, and don't miss the choice of cracking Spanish wines. There is always a great crowd of interesting folk in here. (Spanish Arch, Tel: (091) 561114, Open D, D€€)

● If you need somewhere formal, **The Archway,** at the lower end of Eyre Square, is the smart place in town. This offers good, formal cooking from Regis Martin and his team and the room, whilst small, is always neat and attractive. The food is French-formal and deftly delivered. (3 Victoria Pl, Tel: (091) 563693, Fax: 563074, archway@indigo.ie, Open L&D, L€, D€€€)

● And when the locals need that magical fix of coffee and sweet cake, then there is only **Goya's.** Emer Murray may be the best baker in the country, and her cakes leave everyone in second place: brilliant tiramisu; sublime cheesecake tart; perfect lemon meringue tart. Goya's is also a beautiful, elegant room. (Kirwan's Lane, Tel: (091) 567010, Open daily, L€)

● The **Da Tang Noodle House** is a big local favourite where Catherine O'Brien and her husband Du-Han Tuo show they can make fiery, genuine, no-compromise northern Chinese cooking. It's great fun and great value. (2 Middle St, Tel: (091) 561443 Open L&D, L€, D€)

● For Chinese, go to Charles Chan's up-the-stairs **Royal Villa**, where, if you show you are interested, they will cook real Chinese food for you. Good friendly service, and decent prices too. (13 Shop St, Tel: (091) 563450, Open L&D, L€€, D€€)

● There is more fiery cooking in **The River God Café**, upstairs on Quay Street. They describe their cooking as World French Cuisine, but a fondness for serious spicing with most of the dishes is the dominant theme here. (Tel: (091) 565811 Open L&D, L€€, D€€)

● Much more subtle and enduring is the simple fish cookery in **McDonagh's Seafood House**: fresh fish (which you can also buy) with plenty of spuds and chips. (22 Quay St, Tel: (091) 565001Open L&D, L€, D€) The McDonagh family also run the **Quay Street Wine Bar** – you can show you are in the know by calling it Martine's – and it's a great place to enjoy a range of serious wines. (Tel: (091) 565662 Open L&D, L€, D€)

● **Biquet's** at Spanish Parade is good for bites and a glass of wine, Spanish Parade, Tel: (091) 568450, whilst the new kid in town is the small-but-beautifully-formed **Delight,** at 29 Upper Abbeygate Street, which is where you will find smart sandwiches and hot rolls, Illy coffee and some good sweet baking. (Tel: (091) 567823, Open L, L€)

Out of town:

• **Moran's of the Weir** in Kilcolgan, south of the city, is a legendary tourist haunt but don't let that put you off. The oysters are superb, the rest of the fish cookery pretty well accomplished, and it is a serene and lovely spot for shellfish and a pint. (Kilcolgan, Tel: (091) 796113Open L&D, L€, D€€)

• Richard Casburn's cooking in **Moycullen House Restaurant,** just up the hill from Moycullen village is a delicious complement to this handsome Arts & Crafts House. A good place to eat and stay. (Tel: (091) 555621, Fax: 555566, moyculhs@iol.ie, Open D, D€€. Rates €€)

• The hot destination on the road out to Spiddle is **O'Grady's on the Pier** in Barna. Prices for main dishes can be high, so do what the locals do and choose a collection of starters and you'll get excellent value and good, well-accomplished fish cookery in a nice, cosy, space. (Barna, Tel: (091) 592223 Open L&D, L€, D€€€.

Galway: places to stay

● Dee and Mark Keogh's gorgeous house, **Norman Villa** is as integral a part of Galway as Ti Neatain's pub: if you come to Galway and you don't try to get into Norman Villa, then you haven't really been to Galway. It's a masterpiece of a house, with extraordinary design which shows the owners superb taste. Revel in the delight of the art collection, swoon blissfully in the stylish comfort, and chat to a heap of interesting folk over breakfast. Unmissable. (86 Lwr Salthill, Tel/Fax: (091) 521131, normanvilla@oceanfree.net Rates €€)

● Just around the corner, Berna Kelly's **Devon Dell** is a vivid contrast to the sleekness of Norman Villa; this is cosy Irish vernacular, but the secret of the house is Mrs Kelly's solicitous care, and the great housekeeping and lovely breakfasts. (47 Devon Pk, Lwr Salthill, Tel: (091) 528306, devondell@iol.ie Rates €€)

● On the road to Connemara. Catherine Doyle's beautiful **Killeen House**, at Bushypark is a style-lover's destination: check out the smartness of the house's terrific furnishing. It's also a respite from the bustle of the city. (Killeen, Bushypark, Tel: (091) 524179, Fax: 528065, killeenhouse@ireland.com, killeenhousegalway.com, Rates €€)

● If you need an hotel, then the best choice is the smart new **Radisson SAS**, a couple of minutes' walk from Eyre Square. This hotel is cleverly and artfully designed, and the rooms are very comfortable. (Lough Atalia Rd, Tel: (091) 539300, 538380, radissonsas.com, Rates €€€)

Aran: islands

INIS MOR

On Inis Mor, Treasa Joyce's super **Kilmurvey House** is the destination address: lovely domestic cooking and baking, close to the pristine Kilmurvey beach, close to Dun Aengus, and altogether a great chill-out space. (Kilmurvey Bay, Tel: (099) 61218, Fax: 61397, kilmurveyhouse@eircom.net, kilmurveyhouse.com, Rates €€)

● The cult address on the island is Joelle d'Anjou's clubbish and quite unique **Mainistir House Hostel.** M d'Anjou is a fascinating renaissance man, and a most brilliant vegetarian cook, but some folk find that they don't warm to the aesthetic of the house. For many others it is one of their very favourite places to stay and eat.

(Kilronan, Tel: (099) 61169, Fax: 61351, Rates €)

● For day-time eating, **Joe Watty's** pub, up the hill from Kilronan, is always a good bet. (Kilronan, Tel: (099) 61155, Open L, L€)

INIS OIRR

On little Inis Oirr, Brid Poil's lovely farmhouse in **Radharc an Chlair** is where everyone heads to to chill out. Marvellous cooking from Mrs Poil and the unique atmosphere of this magical island make this house pretty irresistible. This is one of the best-regarded B&B's you will find. (Inis Oirr, Tel: (099) 75019, Rates €)

INIS MAAN

If you take the boat to little Inis Maan, then head for Maureen Concannon's cosy B&B in Moore village, the place where all the Concannons reside. (Inis Maan, Tel: (099) 73019, Rates €)

Connemara: staying

Connemara marries magical beauty with brilliant hospitality. The combination of the two is some sort of bliss altogether, which makes this as desirable a destination as West Cork or the Donegal peninsulas.

● For years, insiders have known that one of the secrets about Connemara is to be a Foyle-watcher. And what's that? Simply someone who keeps an eye on whatever the talented Foyle family, who have been hoteliers in Clifden for generations, are up to.
Well, you are spoilt these days for splendiferous Foyle hospitality. Start with the brilliant Paddy and Julia Foyle in **Quay House,** Clifden. This is, for our money, the most stunningly designed house in the country, with every room a tone poem of good taste and riotous humour. Mix such style with the true hospitality of Paddy and Julia and you have one of the great icon addresses. (Beach Rd, Clifden, Tel: (095) 21369, Fax: 21608, thequay@iol.ie, thequayhouse.com, Rates €€)

● Just down the road, brother Billy has opened up **Dolphin Beach,** a beautiful house with a stunning location on the Sky Road, with great success. This is another dream destination, with great cooking and a true welcome. (Lwr Sky Rd, Tel: (095) 21204, dolphinbeach@iol.free.ie, Rates €€)

Style guru:

Paddy Foyle, what is the secret of making a room comfortable? 'Good mattress, linen and pillows, dark and quiet and with good reading lights.'

● The next generation of Foyles is already at work, for young Mark Foyle is now in charge of **Rosleague Manor,** out towards Letterfrack. It's still early days, but here is another promising Foyle venture in another stylish location. Put this trio together on an itinerary and it's some sort of bliss. (Letterfrack, Tel: (095) 41101, Fax: 41168, rosleaguemanor@ireland.com, Rates €€€)

● And there is more bliss to be found in and around Connemara. If it's country houses you seek, then **Fermoyle Lodge** in Costello, **Garranbaun House** near Letterfrack and **Delphi Lodge,** in a stupendous location at Leenane, are some sort of heaven. All have great cooking and great craic, and drop-dead locations. (Fermoyle Lodge, Costello, Connemara, Tel: (091) 786111, fermoylelodge.com, Rates €€) (Garranbaun House, Moyard, Connemara, Tel: (095) 41649, Fax: 41649, garraunbaun.house@ireland.com, Rates €€) (Delphi Lodge,

Leenane, Tel: (095) 42222, Fax: 42296, delfish@iol.ie, Rates €€€)

● If it's a castle you are after, then there is none better than the gorgeous **Ballynahinch Castle.** This magisterial old pile is brilliantly run by Patrick O'Flaherty and features some superb cooking by chef Robert Webster and his team. If you strike it really lucky, then some happy fisherman will have caught a salmon and it will be on the menu for dinner. Heaven! (Ballinafad, Recess, Tel: (095) 31006, Fax: 31085, bhinch@iol.ie, Rates €€€)

● If you seek splendid isolation and classic cooking, then there is nowhere more calming for the soul than Maire O'Connor's **Lough Inagh Lodge,** on the road between Recess and Kylemore Pass. We would love it if the bedrooms were painted a brighter colour, but this is a distinctive, personal and private little hotel with lovely cooking to be enjoyed in the petite dining room. (Recess, Tel: (095) 34706. Fax: 34708, inagh@iol.ie, Rates €€€)

Connemara – Galway

WHERE TO EAT:

■ **Ballynahinch Castle** is a destination address thanks to Robert Webster's hugely enjoyable country cooking, and a dining room which is one of the most beautiful in the entire country. (see page 77).

■ Locals also eat in the bar at **Lough Inagh Lodge**, or in the dining room if there is a free table. (see page 77).

■ The real destination address here is Hugh and Eileen Griffin's **High Moors** restaurant, a mile outside Clifden. There is nowhere quite like High Moors. The restaurant is actually the sitting room of this pretty bungalow, the food is grown by Hugh in his vegetable plot down the hill and cooked by Eileen on her green Aga in her domestic kitchen, and the flavours will have you clamouring for more after just one bite. You won't get better tasting vegetables and more soulfully moreish desserts anywhere else in Ireland, and with the room packed with locals and holiday-makers who rent cottages around the town, the place will be buzzing. Don't miss it. (Dooneen, Tel: (095) 21342, Open D, D€€)

Gone Fishing

Patrick O'Flaherty, Ballynahinch:
'Here, primarily we fish for wild Atlantic salmon, but there are also brown trout and sea trout. When guests catch a sea trout, they have to throw it back, because it's protected.
'If they catch a salmon, they might also throw it back, but we also prepare a lot of small dinner parties for groups, one of whose members has caught a fish.
'In 2001 the largest fish caught was 16lbs in weight, in 2000 someone caught one weighing 22lbs, and in the past guests have caught fish up to 30lbs. A number of guests enjoy having their salmon smoked and posted to their home address, and some give the fish to their ghillies – and they eat them, or it could be any combination of the above.
'We always cook fresh salmon as simply as possible, either poached or pan fried and baked with a very light sauce, nothing to detract from the fish.
'Do you know why it's called fishing?'
No.
'Because it's not called catching! 'In fact it's not only for the catching that people fish here in the west, it's a much bigger thing than that.'

Staying on the Ring

SCENE OR HERD?

We know, we know: you don't go to the Ring of Kerry. All herd, no scene. A panjandrum of tour buses sardined bumper-to-bumper as they make their way from Killorglin to Kenmare. Traffic jams in all the little towns. Who needs it? Well, you do, frankly. The Ring has many downsides, but it has its upsides as well. And here they are.

If you want to stay in one of the most sublime country houses in Ireland, then David and Geraldine Hare's **Iskeroon** is one of the most gorgeous houses to be found anywhere. You have to cross a beach to get to it, after you have descended down the steepest series of hair-pin bends imaginable, but when you get there the design of this fabulous house will mean that you will never want to leave. It's bliss, but make sure to book for more than one night, otherwise you will die of a broken heart when leaving. (Caherdaniel Tel: (066) 9475119 Fax: 9475488 info@iskeroon.com www.iskeroon.com. Rates €€)

And let's hear it for that great old warhorse, the Great Southern Hotel at Parknasilla. The location is remarkably beautiful, the staff are outstanding (take a bow Sonny, Jackie, Jim and all the crew), the food is rather good, and the collection of modern Irish art is a treat. Check in, and then chill out, and do note that their special offers give very good value for money. The pool means it is a very fine place indeed for the stressed-out parents of young children. (Parknasilla, Tel: (064) 45122 Fax: (064) 45323 info@greatsouthernhotels.com greatsouthernhotels.com, Rates €€€)

Ring of Kerry

RESTAURANTS

• • • • • • • • • • • • • • • • • • •

● Caherciveen: The locals favour the Basque specialities cooked in **QC's** bar in Caherciveen, good, true, imaginative food, much of it char-grilled, overseen by Kate and Andrew Cooke. (3 Main St, Caherciveen, Tel: (066) 9472244, acooke@oceanfree.net, Open L&D L€, D€€)
Two other popular choices in Caherciveen are close to one another on the main street; **Brennan's Restaurant** is admired for its judicious cooking of local foods by Conor Brennan, (Main St, Cahirciveen, Tel: (066) 947 2021, Open D, D€€) whilst **O'Donoghue's Fish Shop and Restaurant** is the place for spankingly fresh fish (the family are in the fish trade) and their own smoked salmon. (Main St, Caherciveen, Tel: (066) 947 2153, Open L&D, L€, D€€)

The Point Bar is another place well-respected by locals for bar food; smart eaters order the fish of the day. (Caherciveen, Tel: (066) 947 2165, Open L&D, L€, D€)

● The other local must-have is the fine, simple food cooked by Anya Carrell and Kevin Mackey at the **Lighthouse Café** on Valentia Island. Check out those views!

● In the higgledy-piggledy town of Killorglin, at the head of the ring, Nick and Anne Foley's famous **Seafood Restaurant and Piano Bar** is one of the liveliest places to eat in Ireland. Come here during race week in Tralee and the place is simply hopping, but the craic is matched by good, unpretentious (and very generous) cooking. (Lwr Bridge St, Killorglin, Tel: (066) 61219, Open D, D€€)

More places to stay:

Mary Gaunt's Victorian House, Caragh Lodge, a few miles south of Killorglin and just inland off the Ring is another well-regarded address. (Caragh Lake, Tel: (066) 976 9115, Fax: 976 9316, caraghl@iol.ie, Rates €€) In Portmagee, there is simple and very inexpensive accommodation in The Moorings, and do try to get a room at the front as the views across to Valentia are ace. (Portmagee, Tel: (066) 947 7108, Fax: 947 7220, moorings@iol.ie, Rates: €)

Kenmare gourmet ghetto

Kenmare has the highest standard of cooking of any town in Ireland, and it's also packed with superb places to stay.

● There is nice, understated food in the long-established **An Leith Phingin,** thanks to Con Guerin's subtle touch with Italian specialities. (35 Main St, Tel: (064) 41559, Open D, D€€)

● Brendan Byrne has taken over the kitchen in Pat Gath's buzzy **d'Arcy's** restaurant, succeeding James Mulchrone. It's still early days and Mr Byrne is still finding his feet, but the room is brilliantly managed by Mr Gath and it's always a great destination. (Main St, Kenmare, Tel: (064) 41589, darcys-kenmare.com, info@darcys-kenmare.com, Open D, D€€)

● Also unmissable is **Jam**, where James Mulchrone makes superb sandwiches and breads and some of the best lunches in town. Don't miss the sausage rolls! (Henry St, Kenmare, Tel: (064) 41591, Open daily, L€)

● Tony Daly runs a good ship in the beautiful **Lime Tree** restaurant, just out front from the Park Hotel. (Shelburne St, Kenmare, Tel: (064) 41225, Fax: 41839, benchmark@iol.ie, Open D, D€€)

● Bruce Mulcahy has a whacky interior in **Mulcahy's** but the food is as disciplined as all get out: great john dory with mussel cream; smashing scallops with red grapes and leeks, magnificent lemon tart, and everything he cooks respects the fundamental rule of flavour. (16 Henry St, Kenmare, Tel: (064) 42383, Open L&D L€, D€€)

Serious Bar Food:

For lunchtime, the hot destination is always The Purple Heather: just try that chicken liver pate, and swoon. The only problem is getting a table. (Henry St, Tel: (064) 41016, Open daily, L€) A lot of locals love the good, hearty food in the Horseshoe Bar, which is always busy. (3 Main St, Tel: (064) 41553, Fax: 42502, Open L&D, L€, D€€) Another favourite local pub is Micky Ned's. And Davitt's is where the locals go for Sunday lunch.

● Kenmare boasts some of the best veterans in the business, none more so than Maura Foley, who has been cooking in the town for 40 years. **Packie's**, is simply outstanding. Simple food, judged to perfection, packed with flavour. (Henry St, Tel: (064) 41508, Fax: 42135, Open D, D€€)

● **The Park Hotel** is where Francis Brennan runs the finest top-class hotel in Ireland. The cooking in The Park is not as ambitious as in the past, but it is always a delight to be in this dining room just to enjoy the superb service and the views.

(Kenmare, Tel: (064) 41200, Fax: 41402, phkenmare@iol.ie, parkkenmare.com, Open D, D€€€. Rates €€€)

● Up in the grand Cascades Restaurant in the grand **Sheen Falls Lodge**, Chris Farrell demonstrates seriously hot culinary talent: loin of rabbit with a Muscat and vanilla dressing; pitch-perfect fresh smoked salmon; superb john dory with artichoke purée. Cascades is also noteworthy for a serious vegetarian menu, and for a magnificent wine list. Pricey, formal, worth every penny. (Kenmare, Tel: (064) 41600, Fax: 41386, info@sheenfallslodge.ie, sheenfallslodge.ie, Open D, D€€€. Rates €€€)

Kenmare where to stay

● As with eating, so with staying: you are spoilt for choice in Kenmare. If you have lots of money and a taste for the good things, then you have to choose between the two best luxury hotels in Ireland. Adriaan Bartels runs the glamorous **Sheen Falls Lodge** with a superb team, and it really does offer sublime luxury and service, with great food in the restaurant. (Kenmare, Tel: (064) 41600, Fax: 41386, info@sheenfallslodge.ie, sheenfallslodge.ie, Open D, D€€€. Rates €€€)

● **The Park Hotel** not only has great style and luxury, it also has Francis Brennan, and Mr Brennan is the greatest hotelier in Ireland. Tough choice. (Tel: (064) 41200, Fax: 41402, phkenmare@iol.ie, parkkenmare.com, Open D, D€€€. Rates €€€)

● For style lovers, the choice is Maura Foley's stunning **Shelburne Lodge**, on the Cork Road. Mrs Foley is the town's greatest cook, and its greatest interior decorator, for Shelburne is a style icon. Don't miss it. (Killowen, Cork Rd, Kenmare, Tel: (064) 41013, Fax: 42135, Rates €€)

● Less stylish, but great destinations, are **Hawthorn House**, smack in the town, and **Sallyport House**, just near the bridge. Hawthorn is a super, cosy B&B, Sallyport a very serene and luxurious house much favoured by visiting Americans.
(Hawthorn House, Shelbourne St, Kenmare, Tel: (064) 41035, Fax: 41932, hawthorn@eircom.net, Rates €€)
(Sallyport House, Glengarrif Rd, Kenmare, Tel: (064) 42066, Fax: 42067, Rates €€)

Scene not herd

Dingle and Killarney are perhaps the two most famous tourist destinations in Ireland, but success has created as many problems for these small towns as it has offered potential. Neither town was built with tour coach travel in mind, yet buses will be bumper to bumper in both during the season. So don't follow the herd: visit them off season, when you can see their delicate beauty.

DINGLE

Dingle is a darling town, with pretty pubs and restaurants, and the drive around the peninsula is one of the most beautiful to be found in Ireland: just be careful to keep your eyes on the road as you head for the peninsula!!

■ The key destination in Dingle is Jim McCarthy's **Chart House Restaurant**, just as you drive into the town travelling west. Perfectly judged cooking from Gary Fitzgerald and Christina Cotter, delightful room management from the boss himself, a great wine list and fantastic ambience add up to the Dingle hot shot, the sort of place where you chill out the very second you walk through the half-door. One of the key Kerry addresses. (The Mall, Tel: (066) 915 2255, charthse@iol.ie, Open D, D€€)

■ **The Captain's House** and **Milltown House** are two of the best of many B&B's to choose from, the former situated right smack in the town, with lovely breakfasts and cosy rooms, the latter a grand house just a little outside town, with stunning views across the bay and the town. Both are superbly run. (The Mall, Tel: (066) 915 1531, captigh@ eircom.net, Rates €€) (Milltown, Tel: (066) 915 1372, Fax: 915 1075, milltown@ indigo.ie, Rates €)

■ Two other choices are the much-loved **Greenmount House**, on Upper John Street, which has fabulous breakfasts, (Tel: (066) 915 1414 Rates €€)

■ And for high rollers the elegantly finished new **Emlagh House** is a super-stylish base, managed by Stella Doyle. (Tel: (066) 915 2345 emlaghhouse.com Rates €€€)

KILLARNEY

• Killarney comes as a disappointment after the magnificence of the lakes, and for many it has become a place to speed through. If you are stopping, then try the cooking in Peppers Bistro in the Killarney Great Southern Hotel, where they still serve classics such as Caesar salad at the table in the silver service style. (Tel: (064) 31262 Open D, D€€)

• Kayne's Bistro, on the edge of town on the Drumhall Hotel offers some pleasing, informal food. (Muckross Rd, Tel: (064) 31431, Open L&D, L€, D€€)

• In town try the stylish modern room of The Cooperage, where the food is fusion-modern, (Old Market Lane, Tel: (064) 37716, Open L&D, L€, D€€) and the traditional fish and shellfish cookery in Gaby's. Look for the famous curragh sign. (27 High St, Tel: (064) 32519, Open D, D€€)

• A retreat from all the tourist fixated bustle can be found in Deenagh Lodge, in the National Park. Joan Greene, influenced by travels in India, cooks imaginatively seasoned vegetarian food in this beautiful old gate lodge. Sit outside enjoying Thali plates, soups and salads. (National Park, Tel: (064) 36274 Open L, L€)

A 4-COURSE MEAL IN THE GREAT SOUTHERN HOTEL IN 1977:

OEUFS POCHES BASQUAISE 90p
Eggs gently poached, served cold on rings of fresh tomatoes, with smoked ham, fresh pepper, pimentos and garlic

TURTUE LADY CURZON 90p
Turtle soup, topped with a curry flavoured cream

CARPETBAGGER STEAK £4.65
Tender fillet, stuffed with fresh Oysters. Served with Green Salad

CREPE COPACCABANA £1.50
Thin Pancakes, filled with Vanilla ice Cream, covered with a hot sweetened Coffee Liqueur. Flavoured in Tia Maria and flamed in Brandy

Taken from 'The Maldon Room' menu, Great Southern Hotel, Killarney, 1977. This same room now houses Peppers Bistro.

East Kerry

CASTLEGREGORY

O'Riordan's Café Friendly service – not always a given in busy Kerry – and good, smart cooking draw the crowds to O'Riordan's.

(Castlegregory, Tel: (066) 713 9379, Fax: 713 9379, Open D, & Sun L, D€€, L€€)

FENIT

The Tankard is a popular place and Adrian O'Sullivan works hard to produce enjoyable and unpretentious food.

(Kilfenora, Fenit, Tel: (066) 713 6164, Fax: 713 6516, sullads@compuserve.com, Open D & Sun L, D€€, L€€)

LISTOWEL

Allo's Bar & Bistro in Listowel is the bar from heaven and the bistro from heaven, and that's even before you lay your head in rooms that seem to have been designed in heaven.

Heavenly Allo's is one of the truly great destinations, and happily one can eat, drink and stay all in the glamorous confines of this sublime space. Helen Mullane and Armel Whyte are one of the great culinary duos in Ireland, and everything they cook, from pitch-perfect fish cookery to their terrific-value-for-money theme nights on Thursdays when they explore the cuisines of the world, is a paragon of pleasure. The bar is sublime.

On no account must you miss this slice of heaven.

(41 Church St, Listowel, Tel: (068) 22880, Open L&D, L€, D€€, Accommodation rates €€€)

TRALEE

Restaurant David Norris

David Norris is a serious cook, which is just what Tralee, a culinarily-underperforming town, needs. His food is exciting: crisp spring roll of shellfish with chilli-garlic butter; fettucine of wild mushrooms with onion velouté sauce; roast fillet of salmon on buttered leeks; crispy confit of duck with chilli-roasted pineapple; frozen liquorice and lime parfait with poached pears. Smart, modern Irish cooking, a pretty room, and excellent value for money.

(Ivy House, Ivy Terrace, Tralee Tel: (066) 718 5654. Open D, D€€)

Kildare: inside track

● **The Ballymore Inn** is one of the most important eating places in Ireland. You might not think this to look at it – it's a simple enough bar and restaurant in the centre of little Ballymore Eustace – but Georgina and Barry O'Sullivan's brilliant cooking demonstrates fanatical attention to detail, both in sourcing their foods – check those bio-dynamic vegetables and leaves – in understanding their food – you could write a history of modern Irish restaurant cooking through analysing their menus – and in cooking and serving their food, which is done with such understatement and consideration that it explains why getting a table here is one of the most difficult tasks in Ireland. The flavours Mrs O'Sullivan conjures are inspiring, nothing less, and we would nominate the meat cookery here as the best in Ireland.
(Ballymore Eustace, Tel: (045) 864585, theballymoreinn@hotmail.com, Open L&D, L€, D€€)

High rollers & hopefuls

Horse racing attracts high rollers and hopefuls to Kildare. The high rollers going to the Curragh will likely stay at the extra-plush Kildare Hotel & Country Club, which also attracts high-rolling golfers. But the reason to head here is for Michel Flamme's very considered and cultured cooking, and for the brilliant wine service by Didier Fiat. M. Flamme has been cooking for many years, but there is a trueness and modesty in his food which belies the swanky nature of the club; he is still interested in making the best food he can, and it shows. (Straffan, Tel: (01) 601 7200, Fax: 601 7299, hotel@kclub.ie, Open D, D€€€, Rates €€€)

Hopefuls, meantime, will be attracted to Marjorie Molloy's rather more modest Tonlegee House, just outside Athy, but it will be the hospitality and the good country cooking which will bring everyone back to this comfortable and pleasing house. Mrs Molloy has the gift of doing things with just the right judgement and nous everytime, and the food, especially breakfast, is excellent. (Athy, Tel/Fax: (0507) 31473, tonlegeehouse@eircom.net Open D, D€€, Rates, €€)

Kilkenny city

● **Cafe Sol**

Kilkenny locals pack out Eavan & Gail's lovely room, opposite the town hall, to enjoy very feminine and poised cooking. Soups, salads, sandwiches, are all beautifully delivered. Happily, during the summer they also open weekend nights.
(William St, Tel: (056) 64987, Open L, L€)

● **Zuni**

Zuni is the happening place in Kilkenny. The restaurant is part of a moody boutique hotel, created by twin sisters Paula and Sandra and their husbands Paul and Alan, which shows considerable elan in both the rooms and the public spaces. The restaurant has already created a major following amongst locals for cooking which is intelligently composed and executed, and has lots of modern verve: blackened chicken Caesar salad; loin of lamb with channa masala; fish 'n' fries. Make sure to order one of the starters served on slates! Recent change of chefs hasn't altered consistency.
(26 Patrick St, Tel: (056) 23999, zuni.ie, Open L&D, L€€, D€€, Rates €€)

● **Pordylos**

Kilkenny locals like the intimate atmosphere of Dermot Dalton and Brian Porteous's restaurant and wine bar. The food is good, service can be unsure.
(The Butter Slip Tel: (056) 70660, Open D€€)

● **Rinuccini Restaurant**

One of the most popular places amongst locals for simple Italian food which is enjoyable and not pricey. Only problem is that it can get mighty crowded. There are also seven well-fitted rooms at decent rates.
(The Parade, Tel: (056) 61575, Open L&D, L€, D€€, Rates €€)

Kilkenny county

● **Calabash** Brian Kelly and Jack Moylan's smashing bistro is tiny and intimate, with right-on-the-money cooking by Mr Moylan and a room with true personality.
(Bennetsbridge Tel: (056) 27850 calabash@eircom.net, Open D, D€€)

● **The Motte** Alan & Tom's restaurant just outside the pretty-as-a-picture town of Inistioge has some funky and eclectic culinary ideas.
(Inistioge, Tel: (056) 58655, Open D, D€€)

● **Oysters** Leo and Sue O'Briens restaurant is a Kilkenny secret, with good simple cooking.
(Thomastown Tel: (056) 54220, Open D€€)

● **Three Sisters** David Kelleher and Eve Bushe are moving their much-loved restaurant to a bigger town, but keep in touch with this smart duo, for they really understand their food and are a team to watch. (Graiguenamanagh Tel: (0503) 24069)

WHERE TO STAY

• **Berryhill**
Belinda and George Dyer's country house is one of the cult addresses in the country. It's furnished with enviable wit and glee, just as you would expect from such a sparky pair. Our fav-ourite is the down-stairs room with the open fire. 7 night stay only.

(Inistioge, Tel: (056) 58434, Fax: 58434, berryhouse.com, info@berryhillhouse.com Rates €)

• **Blanchville House**
Monica Phelan's lovely country house, in Maddoxtown, five miles north of Kilkenny city, is characterised by great comfort and care.
(Maddoxtown, Tel: (056) 27197
info@blanchville.ie, Rates €€)

• **Zuni**
New funky hotel in Kilkenny city (see opposite). (26 Patrick St, Tel: (056) 23999, zuni.ie, Rates €€)

Laois: the inside track

ABBEYLEIX
Preston House

Allison Dowling's restaurant with rooms is as stylish as the beautiful town of Abbeyleix, in which it is the destination address. Great country cooking has a succulence and respect for flavour that is profound, and the rooms are excellent.
(Main St, Tel/Fax: (0502) 31432, Rates €€)

MOUNTRATH
Roundwood House

A few years back, trying to describe what one might do when in Roundwood House, Frank and Rosemary Kennan wrote that "recreation consists mainly of good food, good wine and good conversation". There, in a sentence, you have the heart and soul of this fantastic old house. Bliss.
(Mountrath, Tel: (0502) 32120, roundwood@eircom.net Rates €€)

PORTLAOISE
Ivyleigh House

Dinah Campion's townhouse is one of the most meticulous addresses in Ireland. The cooking, the housekeeping and the hospitality are all utterly benchmark. Guests usually eat dinner in Jim's Kitchen, and also in Pauline Coughlan's **Anapuma** restaurant on Main Street.
(Bank Pl, Tel: (0502) 22081, Fax: 63343, ivyleigh.com, Rates €€)

Jim's Country Kitchen

Jim Tynan's Kitchen is the Portlaoise phenomenon: packed to the rafters at lunchtime, and almost impossible to get into at the weekends when they open for dinner. Great team, great cooking, great fun, excellent value for money. Don't miss it.
(Hynds Sq, Tel: (0502) 62061, Open L&D at weekend, L€, D€€)

Leitrim north to south

● **The Courthouse**

The destination address in north County Leitrim, at the edge of Lough Melvin where Leitrim edges towards the sea, is Piero and Sandra Melis's The Courthouse, in Kinlough.This little restaurant with rooms hoovers up all the local trade for many miles around. Check out the excellent stuffed baby squid, everyone's-favourite calamari, the good pastas and trademark fried courgettes. The rooms are simple and affordable. Guests staying at the McCanney sisters' highly-regarded **Tullaghan House** eat here, and Tullaghan is worth a visit. (Kinlough, Tel: (072) 42391, Open L&D, L€, D€€. Tullaghan, Tel: (072) 41515, emccanney@hotmail.com, €)

● **Holywell**

From Kinlough, travel all the way to the southern edge of the county for Rosaleen and Tom Maher's very lovely and very comfortable Holywell, in Carrick-on-Shannon, a delightful house set just by the bridge and overlooking the river Shannon. Holywell is characterised by a great welcome, a totally-chilled-out atmosphere and a great location if you are boating on the Shannon. Breakfasts are excellent, housekeeping superb. If eating in the town, then do try **The Pyramids,** a little taste of Egypt on the Shannon. (Holywell, Liberty Hill, Tel: (078) 21224, Rates €€) (Carrick-on-Shannon, Tel: (078) 20333, Open D, D€€)

Sustenance on the internet:

Number of results given from google.com on Sunday 26/8/01 in response to the following searches:

• Irish Food:	590,000
• French food:	1,350,000
• English food:	1,650,000
• American food:	1,690,000
• Football:	11,500,000
• Golf:	15,000,000
• Sex:	52,600,000

Limerick: city & county

In the city seek out the alliums: **The Green Onion Caffe** is as individualistic and right on the money as you will get.Great room, great staff and particularly excellent music, mean this is everyone's favourite. (The Old Town Hall Building, Rutland St, Tel: (061) 400710, Open daily L€, D €€) **The Wild Onion,** is a taste of Chicago brought to the market quarter. All day American-style food includes great Chicago burgers, meat patties with French toast, real American cakes and bread all put together right in front of you in their open kitchen. (High St, Cornmarket, Tel: (061) 440055, Open daily, €. wildonioncafe.com)

Dan Mullane's **Mustard Seed** at Echo Lodge is one of the most provocatively beautiful houses in the entire country. This is uniquely stylish and the cooking matches the style all the way. Unmissable. (Ballingarry, Tel: (069) 68508, mustard@indigo.ie, Rates €€€) David Foley's cooking has ensured that the **Wild Geese** continues as the destination restaurant in beautiful Adare, great food, great service. (Adare, Tel: (061) 396451, wildgeese@indigo.ie, Open D€€€) Meanwhile, Con Roche's **Arrabrook** is a huge hit with the locals in Killeline. (Newcastle West, Tel: (069) 61600 arrabrook@eircom.net, Open D, D€€)

Where to stay:

Ballyteigue House: Excellent country cooking and true hospitality explain the abiding success of Margaret Johnson's grand farmhouse. (Rockhill, Tel: (063) 90575, ballyteigue@eircom.net, Rates €€) On the main road south, Tilly Curtin's sweet little Reens Farmhouse is charming; Mrs Curtin takes care of you in just the way you want. (Adagh, Tel: (069) 64276, Rates €€)

Longford: knowledge

● Torc Café

Ruth McGarry-Quinn's lovely cafe and shop is now
three times the size it was when it opened. Eat
the sweet lovelies they bake and make and you'll
understand why the Torc Café is an unstoppable
success story.

This is a great place for good simple lunches of funky
sandwiches, organic pastas, and some of the best sweet baking in
Ireland. Great service. (Ballymahon St, Longford, Tel: (043) 48277,
Open daily, L€)

● The Aubergine Gallery Café

Steve Devlin's up-the-stairs restaurant in the centre of town is where
food lovers head to for some real, true-flavoured modern cooking. It's
a lovely room, with good service from young local folk who enjoy their
work, and the food has lots of style: medallions of beef with four
pepper and herb butter; sesame duck wontons with stir fry vegetables
and hoi sin; aubergine, feta, basil and black olive bruschetta.
(1 Ballymahon St, Tel: (043) 48633, Open D, D€€)

Top five specials from Torc Café:

• Baked Noodle House pasta
with tomato and pepper sauce.

• Warm cheese open sandwich
with Cais Bain cheese, mixed
leaves, sun-dried tomatoes,
pesto dressing.

• Bombay chicken open salad

sandwich, with curried
mayonnaise, grapes and honey.

• Open Brie and Bacon
sandwich with pesto and mixed
leaves.

• Mushroom and Tarragon pasta
with Noodle House pasta.

Louth: old and new

The cooking in Louth can be divided up between the old guard, and the young blades.

● Three talented veterans continue to cook with distinction. In the little village of **Collon,** Des Carroll's **Forge Gallery Restaurant** is a long-time favourite for good country cooking, and it has been a vital out-post for good food for many years. (Church St, Tel: (041) 982 6272, Fax: 982 26584, Open D€€, forgegallery@eircom.net)

● In **Dundalk,** Pat Kerly may well have been at the stoves in the up-the-stairs **Quaglino's** for a long time, but his interest in discovering and creating new ideas with his cooking is undimmed; there is imagination aplenty here. (88 Clanbrassil St, Tel: (042) 933 38567, Fax 932 8598, Open D, D€.) In the little seaside village of **Termonfeckin,** Pat Fox's lovely **Triple House Restaurant** is the place for comfort cooking – Duff's farm mushroom caps with garlic butter; rack of lamb with tomato, oregano and garlic; maternal service, and a truly cosy ambience. (Tel: (041) 982 2616, Open D & Sun L, D€€, L€€)

● The young blades, meantime, man stylish new addresses in Dundalk and Drogheda. In **Dundalk** Susan Heraghty's **No. 32 Restaurant** is a funky modern home for a good cook whose food has acquired a major local following. (Market St, Tel: (042) 933 1113, Open L&D, L€, D€€.) **Café Metz** on Francis Street is as popular as ever (Francis St, Dundalk, Tel: (042) 933 9106, Open L&D, L€, D€.) Also in Dundalk, the **Windsor Bar** has a good restaurant upstairs. (Dublin St, Tel: (042) 38146, Open L & D, L€, D€€)

● In **Drogheda,** meantime, the **Keyside Café Bar** has the sort of eclectic modern menus that draw in ideas and influences from all over the globe, so expect anything and everything from lemon grass and

chilli mussels to hot Annagassan smoked salmon with citrus vinaigrette. The food here is also good value.
(The Mall, Tel: (041) 984 4878, Open L & D, L€, D€)

CARLINGFORD

Carlingford has become the food lovers destination in Louth. A handsome, sensitively maintained little coastal town, it is a darling place to escape to for a weekend.

● Your key address is the Carroll family's smashing **Ghan House:** lovely new rooms, great cooking at the weekends, and this is where all the action is happening right now, so you will need to book well in advance. (Tel: (042) 937 3682, Open D, D€€)

● In the town itself, Mark Wood's **Kingfisher Bistro** is the hot location for excellent savoury cooking and the true Carlingford craic. (Tel: (042) 937 3716, Open D, D€€)

● Right in the centre of town, Brian McKevitt's **The Oystercatcher** is a fun choice, with great service from the boss and nice rooms at decent prices. (Market Sq, Tel:

(042) 937 3922, Fax: 937 3987, bmckev@eircom.net. Open D, D€€. Accommodation €€)

● There are very comfortable room also in **Beaufort House,** where Michael and Glynis Caine reveal the professionalism that marks them out as former restaurateurs. (Ghan Rd, Tel: (042) 937 3879, Fax: 937 3878, mcaine@beauforthouse.net, Rates €€)

● Many folk take lunch in **Georgina's Bakehouse;** check out the soups and those gingerbread men. (Tel: (042) 937 3346, Open daily, L€)

● And do have a drink or two in **O'Hare's** pub, and in **Lily Finnegan's** pub in Whitestone.

Mayo: & Achill Island

● **Newport House** is the very archetype of what you
want a country house to be: it is grand, formal,
traditional, the cooking is excellent, the wine list
amazing, the service an echo of silver-service days. For
Mayo locals, it remains the ultimate big night out
destination. Newport, Tel: (098) 41222, Fax: 41613, Rates €€€.) In
Newport itself, **Kelly's Kitchen,** an offshoot of the splendid
butcher's shop, is great for tasty simple food. (Main St, Tel: (098)
41647, Open daily L& early D, L€, D€) If you are holidaying in this
region, then consider Louisa and Alan Stoney's **Rosturk Woods**,
where there is both B&B and also some self-catering accommodation,
in a glorious location.
(Mulrany, Tel: (098) 36264, stoney@iol.ie, Rates €€)

● In Westport, locals choose between the ever-reliable **Quay
Cottage**, (The Harbour, Tel: (098) 264512, Open L&D, L€, D€€) and
Robbie McMenamin's the **Lemon Peel**.
(The Octagon, Tel: (098) 26929, Open D, D€€)

● Right on the southern border, **Echoes** in Cong is a terrific family-
run restaurant, with exceptional meat cookery, again from the family
butcher next door. (Main St, Tel: (092) 46059, Open D€€)

Achill Island:

On beautiful Achill, the
choices in Keel are
between:
• **Calvey's**
(Tel: 098-43158, Open
L&D), where you should
try Achill lamb.

• The **Boley House**,
(Tel: 098-43147 Open
D) still doing the
business after thirty
years. Great salmon in
season.

• The Joyce family's
The Beehive
(Tel: 098-43134, which

has nice handmade
food and good views
from the patio.

• The Hassett family's
The Chalet,
(Tel: 098-43157, Open
D) where the best
choice is the fresh fish
of the day. (All €-€€)

Meath: the inside track

Kieron Thompson, Newport House (see left)

'The reason I first came to Newport, was because they always had a good value wine list. Now I like to sell the vintage wines I have in my cellar at the same price as they would be found wholesale in London. I'll never be able to replace these wines, their prices have risen stratospherically. I have an old list, that predates my time here, where Chateau Latour sells at £3, but Mateus Rose sells at £1.20. The Mateus has risen with inflation, but the Latour has risen exponentially.'

● Many years ago, the finest food cooked in Ireland was cooked in County Meath, the work of the late Catherine Healy, at Dunderry Lodge. Today, the best cooking in Meath comes from one of her pupils, for in the charmingly aged **Boltown House,** Susan Wilson shows that she learnt well at Dunderry. Her country cooking is precise and alive with provocative flavours and textures.
(Kells, Tel: (046) 43605, Fax: 43036, boltown@iolfree.ie, Rates, €€)

● Another great Meath address is Niamh Colgan's splendid B&B, **The Olde Workhouse.** Yes, it can be hard, as you weave your way through the fantastic breakfast that Niamh prepares, to believe that this imposingly grand building was ever a workhouse. Today, it is devoted to comfort, and it is a great destination. Dunshaughlin, (Tel: (01) 825 9251, comfort@a-vip.com, Rates €€)

● **Boyle's Tearooms** on the main street of Slane is a timeless spot for tea and sandwiches, (Main St, Tel: (041) 24195, Open L&D, L€, D€).Eastwards on the coast at Bettystown, **Bacchus at the Coastguard** is a popular restaurant which appropriately specialises in fish cookery.
(Bayview, Bettystown, Tel: (041) 982 8251, Fax: 982 8236, Open D & Sun lunch, D€€€, L€€)

Monaghan knowhow

● The rooms in **Hilton Park** are glorious and grand, indeed their scale is almost intimidating. But Johnny and Lucey Madden's bonhomie brings this behemoth of a place down to real life. The cooking is amongst the best found in the country houses, and breakfasts in the return of the basement kitchen are superlative; don't miss the scrambled eggs, don't miss the gardens.
(Clones, Tel: (047) 56007, Fax: 56033, jm@hiltonpark.ie, hiltonpark.ie, Rates €€€)

● The other grand space around the border making a mark recently has been Sammy Leslie's **Castle Leslie**, in Glaslough, thanks to the presence of Noel McMeel in the kitchen. Mr McMeel is one of the most naturally talented chefs cooking today, and dinner here can be perfect: roast corn soup with cumin; confit of duck done Asian-style with pak choi with a port and balsamic reduction; expertly seasoned fillet of beef with oyster mushrooms; delicious panna cotta with strawberry and black pepper ice cream. This is mature and convincing cooking and it is attracting a serious audience. The castle itself is being steadily improved by Sammy Leslie and her team. (Glaslough, Tel: (047) 88109, Fax: 88256, ultan@castle-leslie.ie, castleleslie.com, Open D, D€€€. Accommodation €€€)

● Another talented chef is Raymond McArdle, who made a great reputation cooking at Deane's in Belfast, and has taken over the kitchens at the popular **Nuremore Hotel,** south of Carrickmacross. Mr McArdle cooks only for the restaurant and his ambitions are serious. (Carrickmacross, Tel: (042) 966 1438, Fax: 966 1853, nuremore@eircom.net, nuremore-hotel.ie, Open L&D, L€€, D€€€)

Sligo: the inside track

● Moira and Christy Tighe's **Cromleach Lodge** is far and away the outstanding restaurant in County Sligo. This is a passionate, devoted team of female chefs who display great sympathy and savvy in their cooking. The rooms are excellent, also, with stunning views, and whilst the decor leaves folk divided for and against, the cooking convinces everyone. Above all, don't miss the desserts, which are superlative. (Castlebaldwin, Tel: (071) 65155, Fax: 65455, cromleach.com, Rates €€€)

● On the road north out of Sligo, **La Vecchia Posta**, hard by the side of the road in Cliffoney, is another good destination, for excellent pastas and other implicitly-understood Italian food. (Tel: (071) 76777, Open D€€)

● Sligo has two of the best country houses in Sandy and Deb Perceval's stupendous **Temple House**, in Ballymote, a gargantuan old house on 1,000 acres. It's a special place, a house where everyone is quickly your new best friend. Great cooking from Deb Perceval also. (Ballymote, Tel: (071) 83329, Fax: 83808, templehouse.ie, Rates €€. *NB Host very allergic to scented products. Please enquire when booking)* In Riverstown, Brian and Anne O'Hara's resplendent **Coopershill** is one of the most meticulously maintained country houses you can find. The housekeeping is superlative, the hospitality likewise. Parties of friends love to book Coopershill for country house weekends off-season. (Riverstown, Tel: (071) 65108, Fax: 65466, coopershill.com, Rates €€€)

● In Sligo town itself, **Bar Bazaar** on Market St and **Eurobar** on the Stephen's Street car park are good places for coffee, and don't miss the sublime **Hargadon's bar**, in the centre of town.

Tipperary: knowledge

BALLINDERRY

Brocka-on-the-Water is one of Tipp's great secret surprises. Anne and Anthony Gernon's restaurant is in their house, and they decorate their few tables with domestic designs, and they cook in a style which we might say reveals the glory of domestic cooking; garden vegetables; the best beef you can eat; the best wild game in season, the creamiest desserts. It's a sublime adventure to eat here, but make sure to book in advance as it's a tiny space. (Kilgarvan Quay, Ballinderry, Tel: (067) 22038, Open D, D€€)

CASHEL

Chez Hans has been the benchmark restaurant of busy Cashel for over three decades, and today young Jason Matthiae maintains the terrific standard which this beautiful, converted church has always enjoyed. Seafood cookery is always perfect, but do order a rare steak; it will gladden the heart of the chef (they like their meat well done around here) and you will get a taste of superb midlands beef. Fantastic room. (Cashel, Tel: (062) 61177, Open D, D€€€)

● Just around the corner, there is more great cooking in **Legends Restaurant,** and a dining room from which you look out and up straight at the Rock of Cashel. Michael and Rosemary O'Neill are a great team, and service and the spot-on food are just right. Book one of the simple rooms and you can order that extra bottle of wine and make a true trip to Tipp. (The Kiln, Cashel, Tel: 9062) 61292, legendsguesthouse.com, info@legendsguesthouse.com, Open D, €€. Accommodation Rates €€)

● A favourite room in the centre of Cashel is the excellent **Spearman** restaurant. The food here may appear simple, but it is

WHERE TO STAY

- **Ashley Park House,** just outside Nenagh, is a favourite house, run with great calm by Margaret Mounsey. Lovely serene lakeland. (Nenagh, Tel: (067) 38223, Fax: 38013, davidmackenzie@compuserve.com, Rates €€)

- **Inch House**, close to Thurles, is an excellent restaurant with fine accommodation at very good prices. Don't miss their fruit loaf, whatever you do. (Thurles, Tel: (0504) 51261, Fax: 51754, inchhse@iol.ie, Open D€€, Rates €€)

- There is great hospitality and some very fine food at **Annagh Lodge**, Rachel and Andrew Stirling's very-child-friendly house at Coolbawn. (Coolbawn, Tel: (067) 24225, annaghlodge.com, Rates €€)

prepared and cooked with true TLC and is utterly delicious, which makes the Spearman an invaluable lunchtime destination and a great respite from the ravages of the main N8 road. (97 Main St, Cashel, Tel: (062) 61143, Open L&D, L€, D€€)

CAHIR

In Cahir, Michael and Deirdre Clifford draw in the crowds to their upstairs room, **Clifford's at The Bell,** above the pub of that name, just set back from the main square. Mr Clifford is one of the great Irish cooks, and his judgement and culinary precision never falter: do try the gateau of Clonakilty black pudding and the chicken with Milleens cheese, two of his most famous creations. (Cahir, Tel: (052) 43232, Open D & Sun L, L€€, D€€)

CLONMEL

O'Tuama's Café is the most popular room in town, packed out at lunchtime with smart locals who love the excellent sandwiches and soups, the spot-on dishes of the day such as crunchy Thai chicken salad or excellent sirloin steak bruschetta, and the walk-a-country-mile-for-them desserts. If you have given up on banoffi pie, then O'Tuama's exists to restore your faith in this much-maligned classic dessert, but every sweet thing made here is treasureable. (Market Place, Clonmel, Tel: (052) 27170 Open L, L€)

Tipperary

● Just across from O'Tuama's, there is some nice cooking in Declan Gavigan's **Mr Bumbles** restaurant and this is a popular evening destination. (Kickham St, Clonmel, Tel: (052) 29188, Fax: (052) 29380, Open L&D, L€, D€€)

● Another favourite room is Angela Ryan's **Angela's Restaurant**, where this sparky Aussie cooks fine salads and savoury dishes. (14 Abbey St, Clonmel, Tel: (052) 26899, Open L, L€)

NENAGH
Peter and Mary Ward's café in their legendary **Country Choice** deli is the destination, for home-made Irish cooking with true succulence and savour. The Wards truly understand food, and their knowledge shines through in pure flavours and exciting tastes, whatever they cook. (25 Kenyon St, Nenagh, Tel: (067) 32596, countrychoice.com, Open L, L€)

● Just up the street, don't miss the splendid **Gleeson's Tea Rooms,** for tea and a bun. It hasn't changed a jot in decades, and long may it remain the same. (37/38 Mitchell St, Nenagh, Tel: (067) 31518, Open L, L€)

Local secrets:

• In Killaloe, Gooser's is popular for fish dishes in a busy pub. (Killaloe, Tel: (061) 376791)

• In Terryglass, everyone goes to The Derg Inn for Sunday lunch (Terryglass, Tel: (067) 22037, Fax: 22297, derginn@eircom.net)

• In Thurles, don't miss the fantastic brews in Dwan's Brew Pub, a stylish, swish room which is home to one of the country's best micro-breweries. (Thurles, Tel: (0504) 26007)

• For reliable on-the-road food, Matt the Thresher at Birdhill, on the main road to Limerick, is an ever-reliable institution. (Birdhill, Tel: (061) 379227)

• In Puckane, try Kennedy's pub for a pint of Guinness as it used to be before Diageo made it into an alcoholic popsicle.

West Waterford

You can trust us on this: West Waterford is a food lover's paradise, but as yet few people are aware of this delicious fact. Paradise, and unspoilt. Double paradise. Here is a place to linger, a major new destination for the food lover.

● **Buggy's Glencairn Inn** is the place responsible for making Glencairn – which is frankly a wide spot in the road – into one of the food lover's most treasured places to stay and eat. Ken and Cathleen Buggy run the most idiosyncratic and inspiring pub, restaurant and place to stay you will find anywhere. The food is unlike anyone else's cooking (we're sure Mr Buggy improvises with every dish), the bar is a haven, the rooms are sublime and enchanting, and dinner and accommodation are great value. People have tears in their eyes leaving here (and that is no exaggeration). (Tel: (058) 56232 Fax: 56232 www.lismore.com buggysglencairninn@eircom.net, Open D, D€€, Rates €€)

● Just outside the pretty village of Cappoquin, Paul Deevy is currently cooking the food of his life in the elegantly modest **Richmond House.** With his young assistant, Maria Wall, this fine cook is turning out amongst the best country house cooking you can eat in Ireland: cassoulet of fresh monkfish and Rossmore mussels; crispy confit of duck leg on pickled cucumber; roast rack of west Waterford lamb on creamed Puy lentils; pan seared Dunmore East scallops with fresh pasta. The rooms are cosy and understated, the service maternal and relaxing. A great destination. (Tel: (058) 54278 Fax: 54988 www.richmondhouse.net info@richmondhouse.net, Open D, D€€, Rates €€)

West Waterford

● In **Hanora's Cottage** in the lovely Nire Valley near Clonmel the Wall family go from strength to strength to strength. Eoin Wall and his wife Judith have taken charge in the kitchens and so Hanora's is not just a place to stay but also a destination restaurant in its own right. Mary and Seamus Wall, Mum and Dad, meantime continue to create one of the most magnificent breakfasts in the country, and Hanora's is some sort of special enchantment. Walkers love it. Hell, everyone loves it. (Nire Valley, Clonmel, Tel: (052) 36134 Fax: 36540 hanorascottage@eircom.net www.hanorascottage.com, Open D, D€€, Rates €€)

● In Dungarvan, Paul and Maire Flynn's **Tannery Restaurant** offers some of the most cutting-edge cooking found in these islands. Hugely disciplined and creative, Mr Flynn is a master chef, a man who can make bacon and cabbage into a culinary art form, and indeed his creations with Irish staples are amongst the most distinguished cooking found in any restaurant. And whatever you do don't miss his great theme desserts. Gorgeous dining room.
(Tel: (058) 45420 Fax: 45518, tannery.ie info@tannery.ie Open L & D, L€€. D€€€)

Great pub food:

• You will find clever and delicious cooking from Eoin Madden in Madden's bar in Lismore, food so good that it's a crime to call it pub food: chicken and chorizo paella with saffron rice; lamb kebabs with couscous and a tomato and cucumber salad; lemon risotto with grilled herby mushrooms. Fresh breads, organic ingredients and soothing piano player whilst you eat adds up to the pub food from heaven.

•More conventional bar food, in a charming room, can be found just down the road in Eamonn's Place: braised beef with sweet carrots and floury mashed potatoes; baked cod; a lemon meringue pie to finish.

•In Dungarvan, smart locals eat lunch in The Parish Bar, where the staff take their simple food very seriously and produce it with great care. This is good cooking, with fresh ingredients and real imagination.

West Waterford

● There are great desserts also in **White Horses**, Christine Power's simple, single room restaurant in the little village of Ardmore. Sweet things may be the speciality here – they make a tiramisu you would walk a country mile to eat – but there is generosity and care in the savoury cooking also – monkfish tail with a chablis velouté; beef tournedos with a beurre maitre d'hotel; tagliatelle with asparagus – and the room, on a warm summer day, is cosseting and charming. Quite lovely. (Admore, Tel: (024) 94040, Open L&D, L€, D€€)

● **An Carn**, in Ring, is a newcomer, but Deuglan and Siobhan O'Reagain have confidence and charm and the combination of the simple rooms and the very polished cookery in the restaurant have made this a hot new destination. Lovely fish cookery and outstanding desserts from Siobhan are some sort of bliss, and food and accommodation are very keenly priced. Make sure to get a room at the front, and just drool at that sunrise as an orange sun rises from out of the sea! Great spot for Sunday lunch.
(Ring, Dungarvan, Tel: (058) 46611, Fax: 46614, ancarn@eircom.net, ancarn.com, Open D & Sun L, D€€, L€, Accommodation €€)

● **Gortnadiha House** is a little further down the steep hill of Ring, and Eileen Harty runs a superbly hospitable B&B. Gortnadiha is lovely; a massive fire blazing in the sitting room makes you want to sit right down and not get up. Breakfasts are long and leisurely, the rooms are beckoning. (Ring, Dungarvan, Tel: (058) 46142, ringcheese@eircom.net, Rates €€)

● **Powersfield House** is newly opened, but Eunice Power's superb eye for interior and exterior decorating has already made this a cult address in West Waterford. Eunice also cooks in Powersfield's restaurant at the weekends: the local joke is that Eunice accomplishes so much that there really has to be two of her. (Ballinamuck West, Dungarvan, Tel: (058) 45594, Fax: 45550, Rates: €€)

East Waterford

● In Tramore, **Pat Hartley's Bistro** is a popular choice with the holidaymakers who continue to come to this resort town (Tel: 051-390888 Open D, D€€), whilst the hot new arrival in this region is **Isaac's Apple,** east of Tramore in the village of Fennor, on the road to Annestown, where Michael and Sheena Burns' upstairs dining room (above Mother McHughes pub) offers onion and linseed crusted pork fillet; pan-fried butterfish; sirloin with straw potatoes and lots of clever and considered cooking which has made their reputation. They plan to relocate to Tramore in the future, so check that first. (Tel: (051) 391489, Open D, D€€)

● And in Annestown itself, John and Pippa Galloway run a splendid country house in the romantic **Annestown House.** This region is unspoilt and largely unexplored (aside from Tramore itself!) and Annestown is a great base for getting to know the coastline. (Tel: (051) 396160 Fax: 396474, annestown.com, Rates, €€)

Great pub food:

• The destination in Cheekpoint is Mary and Dunstan McAlpin's terrific Suir Inn.
This is a chill-out comfy pub, with some of the most delicious food you will find in the region, and one's only regret is that it isn't open at lunchtime. But, for a simple dinner of delicious seafood, with a couple of cool, relaxing pints, this is a dream place to drive the seven miles from Waterford city.
(Tel: (051) 382220

cheekpoint@tinet.ie Open D, D€€)

• Down in Dunmore East, The Ship retains its status as the favourite place to eat for the many holidaymakers who come here year after year. It's a busy, bustling fun place to come to, especially in summertime when the relaxed style suits summer spirits, but like McAlpin's this is pub food with ambition, and very good it is too.
(Tel: (051) 383141 Fax: 383144 Open L&D, L€, D€€)

Waterford City

Food & wine:

David Dennison's Wine Vault, on High Street, is a masterly combination of good cooking, a superb selection of wines, and a very welcoming, clubbable room. It's always a treat to be walking through those doors, even if you only intend to buy a couple of bottles of wine. Smart locals always drink what the boss advises, and indeed the special wine and food menus devised by the boss are often the very best things to choose here.
(Waterford, Tel: (051) 853444 Fax: 853777
bachus@eircom.net, Open L&D, L€€, D€€)

● Martin Dwyer's eponymous restaurant on Mary Street, **Dwyer's of Mary Street,** has been confidently redesigned in recent times, and offers very professional cooking and service, with assured, restrained food in a pleasingly restrained atmosphere.
Tel: (051) 8577478 Open D, D€€.

● Outside the town, the very talented Michael Quinn is chef at the rather grand **Waterford Castle Hotel**, and aside from the food it's fun to take the ferry across to this private estate.
Tel: (051) 878203 Fax: 879316,
info@waterfordcastle.com, waterfordcastle.com, Rates €€€.

● Cornelius and Sue O'Grady have serious ambitions for their eponymous restaurant with rooms, **O'Grady's**, on the Cork road just down the hill from the Waterford crystal factory. Ingenious dishes such as lobster and asparagus salad, ruddy things such as scallops with bacon and champ or roast hake Provençale show good judgement and maturity. Their comfortable rooms also make this a good overnight destination. Cork Rd,
Tel: (051) 378851, Fax: 374062, Open L & D, L€, D€€.

Westmeath: chillout

ATHLONE

Mary and Annie's **Left Bank Bistro** is the Midlands hot spot. Since moving down the hill to Fry Place (good address girls!) this restaurant has just gotten better and better: the food has become  ever-more assured and delicious and the sheer affection in which this restaurant is held by the folk of Athlone is gladdening to the heart. It's a beautiful room – designed by Ann-Marie O'Neill, with food to match: roast chicken with Tuscan bean mash; pork fillet with Shanghai noodles; chicken wings with Thai sweet chilli dip; char-grilled halibut. Don't miss it.

(Fry Pl, Athlone, Tel: (0902) 94446, Fax: 94509, leftbank@isite.ie, leftbankbistro.com, Open L&D, L€, D€€)

● The paper tablecloths and the crayons for the kiddies in **Tribeca** signal its sharp family focus. Good pizzas and all round friendly food explain its success. (1 Abbey Lane, Tel: (0902) 98805, Fax: 91954, seananduna@eircom.net, Open D, D€€)

GLASSON

Ray and Jane's **Wineport** is another Midlands Don't Miss! This inspiring restaurant is in the process of adding new rooms as we write, which will make it even more of a chill-out space. The dining

The two great Midlands institutions are:

• Steven and Martina Linehan's Le Chateau, down on the river in Athlone, a bustling, theatrical room (St Peter's Port, Athlone, Tel: 0902-94517, Fax: 93040, lechateau@eircom.net Open D & Sun L, D€€, L€€)

• Noel Kenny's Crookedwood House, a few miles outside Mullingar, a fine house which also has a good restaurant. (Crookedwood, Tel: (044) 72165, Fax: 72166, cwoodhse@iol.ie, Open D, D€€)

Spa cuisine:

'It's just lighter than regular food, with light sauces, no cream and butter, and quite a few vegetarian dishes,' says Bernadette Fagan of her Spa Cuisine. A typical meal would be: sweetcorn and ricotta roulade, with chilli jam; lentil loaf with mango chutney; raspberry and honey crème fraîche pots, with an oatmeal topping.

room hard by the lake side is gorgeous, the service is meticulous and the food always pleasing and deftly delivered. Brilliant. (Glasson, Tel: (0902) 85466, Fax: 85471, wineport.ie, restaurant@wineport.ie, Open L&D, L€, D€€)

● There is good informal eating in Simon Grogan's bar, **Grogan's,** in Glasson. (Glasson, Tel: 0902-85158, Open L&D, L€, D€€)

MOATE

The chill-out capital here is, without a doubt, the unique **Temple Country House** and spa. Bernadette and Declan Fagan's house is the most magnificent spa in Ireland, not because it's slick and expensive, but because it is totally dedicated to giving its guests total TLC. The cooking is also superb, the rooms quite lovely, and this is a fantastic address. (Horseleap, Moate, Tel: (0506) 35118, Fax: 35008, templespa.ie, Rates €€)

MULLINGAR

The Belfry Therese Gilsennan is one of the best known cooks in the Midlands, and has taken up the stoves at this spanking new, beautifully converted church. (Ballynegall, Tel: (044) 42488 belfryrestaurant@eircom.net. Open D & late Sun L, D€€, L€€)

● Great home baking and cooking from the Gray sisters is the keynote of **Gallery 29 Café**, a hit with smart locals. (Oliver Plunkett St, Tel: (044) 49449, corbetstown@eircom.net, Open daily, L€)

Wexford: eating

Seriously Good Pub Food can be found south of Wexford:

● The popular destination in Kilmore Quay, right on the south coast, is Kehoe's pub: good seafood cookery. (Kilmore Quay, Tel: (053) 29830, Fax: 29820, Open daily, L & early D, L€, D€€)

● In Carne (called Carnsore Point on road maps) the hugely popular Lobster Pot bar is reliable and locals appreciate good food being served throughout the day.
(Carne, Tel: (053) 31110, Fax: 31401, Open L&D, L€-€€, D€-€€)

ROSSLARE

Eugene Callaghan's cooking in **La Marine Bistro** is a definition of icon cooking. The room is glam and gorgeous, service is awesomely good, and the food is nothing less than amazing, a chef of great skill and maturity at the height of his powers. Don't miss the duck confit, don't miss the chilli squid; hell, go early and often, for this is some of the most singular cooking in Ireland.
(Rosslare, Tel: (053) 32114, Fax: 32222, kellyhot@iol.ie, kellys.ie, Open L&D, L€, D€€)

WEXFORD

Everyone's favourite in Wexford town recently has been **Heaven's Above**, a restaurant above the atmospheric the Sky and the Ground pub which chef Liam Forde put on the map. Mr Forde has moved on to his own place, Forde's on the Crescent, but the food in Heaven's Above remains well above normal pub food standards which means it is still a buzzy place.
(112/113 Sth Main St, Tel: (053) 21273, Fax: 21832, Open D & Sun L, D€€. L€€)

● In **Forde's**, meantime, Liam Forde is once again building an appreciative audience for his

wise, flavourful cooking and it's great to see the chef in his own space.
(The Crescent Quay, Tel: (053) 23832 Fax: 23832, Open D, D€€)

● Tess Smith's is currently cooking in the **Wexford Arts Centre Cafe**, at Cornmarket, and producing some amazingly ambitious food; blackened salmon with couscous; seared beef noodle salad, fantastic frangipane tarts, and delicious filled ciabattas. It's not a great location, but here is cooking to savour. Note, they also offer a catering service. (Cornmarket, Tel: (053) 23764, Open L)

● Roberto Pons' **La Dolce Vita**, at the Westgate, is a pretty room and some of this Italian food can hit the spot. (Westgate, Tel: (053) 23935, Open D, D€€)

● **La Riva**, above the newsagents on The Crescent, is a long-time Wexford favourite for flavourful, straightforward cooking. (Crescent Quay, Tel: (053) 24330, Open D, D€€)

Kelly's Resort Hotel: The stats

■ In 1976, a bottle of Sancerre 1970 cost £2.75, whilst Chateau Cheval Blanc 1960 – one of France's cult wines – would have set you back a wapping £4.60.

■ In 1972 William J Kelly offered a fully inclusive "Your health deserves a break" package with weekends costing £8, and a six-day holiday just £14.15 per person.

■ Today, the chefs in Kelly's produce, on average, one thousand meals per day.

■ The record for regular visitors to Kelly's goes to Mr and Mrs Robert L Keogh, who holidayed in Kelly's for more than half a century.

(From 'The Book of Kelly's')

Wexford: staying

● **Kelly's Resort Hotel** in Rosslare is, quite simply, Parent Heaven. There is no other place where your little emperors are so well looked after and where, as a consequence, you can chill out so thoroughly. But be warned; you need at least a five day break to work out all that tension, and also to enjoy Jim Aherne's smashing food, to explore the singular wine list, and to come to know Bill Kelly's outstanding art collection. Bliss.
(Rosslare, Tel: (053) 32114, Fax: 32222, kellyhot@iol.ie, kellys.ie, Rates €€€)

● There is more bliss just outside Enniscorthy, where Jane and Gordon Parker's fantastic **Salville House** is one of the great country house addresses. It's bohemian, it's unique, and Gordon Parker's cooking is brilliant: seared scallops with salad; Thai-style soup with monkfish and prawns and cellophane noodles; breast of chicken with coriander and chilli and roasted vegetables; passion fruit caramel with crème anglaise. This is as good as country house cooking gets, and it makes Salville a true icon address.
(Enniscorthy, Tel/Fax: (054) 35252, salvillehouse.com salvillehouse@eircom.net, Rates €€)

● A little further south, we love the wild hospitality of Mary Keogh in the little bungalow B&B that is **Vale View**, just off the main road, (St John's, Enniscorthy, Tel: 054-35262, Rates €) whilst in Wexford the favourite address is Seamus and Kay **McMenamin's Townhouse,** on Auburn Terrace, just across from the railway station. Excellent breakfasts, some interesting beds, though some rooms could perhaps be smartened up a little at this stage.
(3 Auburn Tce, Redmond Rd, Wexford, Tel: 9053) 46442, mcmem@indigo.ie, Rates €€)

Wicklow: a to b

● **Avoca Handweavers** is a dream made real. The dream? To cook food for hundreds of folk every day which is imaginative, real and consistent. The reality? In Kilmacanogue, in Powerscourt (and in Dublin) the Avoca Chain manage to do that, to the delight of their adoring fans (Avoca doesn't have customers). The Pratt family's inspired cafés have a true culture of cooking which means this is food cooked with skill and understanding, and the result is purest deliciousness. You will have to queue, but so what? (Kilmacanogue, Tel: (01) 286 7466, Fax: 286 2367, avoca.ie, Open L, L€-€€)

● **Brook Lodge Inn.** Here is another dream made real in Wicklow. The dream? To build a country hotel with a benchmark restaurant from scratch, just an hour from Dublin. The reality? The Brook Lodge Inn and its Strawberry Tree restaurant are the most exciting new arrivals in Ireland's food and hospitality culture. Evan Doyle and his partner Frieda Wolfe hit the ground running when they opened their doors, and the Brook Lodge is now beloved by folk grabbing a night away from the city, by weekday business folk who have conferences here, by food lovers who adore the cutting-edge cookery in the restaurant, and by

The Avoca stats:

Average number of eggs used per week in Avoca Handweavers Café, Kilmacanogue?

'Three thousand, two hundred and forty.'

Wicklow

weekenders, who love to come here for the organic markets they hold every month. It's a brilliant concept, the Brook Lodge, but who could ever have believed the reality would be so pristine. Unmissable. (Macreddin Village, Tel; (0402) 36444, Fax: 36580, brooklodge@macreddin.ie, brooklodge.com, Open L&D, L€€, D€€€, Rates €€€)

BRAY
The **Tree of Idleness** is one of the most special restaurants in the country. Susan Courtellas and manager Tom Monaghan are a dream team for hospitality, the Greek-Cypriot cookery is fabulous – you will find tastes here that can't be found anywhere else – and the totality of the experience that is dinner in the Tree is hard to match. Fantastic wine list, great place. And do ask Mr Monaghan's help to navigate your way to one of the numerous, fantastic treats listed here.
(Sea Front, Bray, Tel: (01) 286 3498, Fax: 282 8183, Open D, D€€€)

DUNLAVIN
Rathsallagh House is a favourite for well-heeled Dubliners (and golfers) who like to get away to the O'Flynn's big, handsome house and resort to recover from the gridlock of Dublin. Breakfasts are lengthy and languourous, dinner is noble country cooking, the away-from-it-all ambience more than justifies the high prices. (Dunlavin, Tel: (045) 403112, Fax: 403343, info@rathsallagh.com, rathsallagh.com, Rates: €€€)

GREYSTONES
Pat Keown is a great wine buff, and maintains a serious cellar at the **Hungry Monk,** one of those (happily) changeless Wicklow restaurants where people get exactly what they want and exactly what they like. Prawns and scallops with garlic butter, 16oz steaks ('no 8oz-10oz or any of that racket' says Pat), half roast duck, sumptuous crab salads. Sunday lunch – or Linner, as they call it – lasts from mid-day to 8pm, and is a local legend in the area (see right). Recently they have opened a wine bar downstairs, serving cod in a real

beer batter, home-made hamburgers, Thai-style goujons of chicken, goat's cheese bruschetta. Not surprisingly, it's full every night.
(Greystones, Tel: (01) 287 5759, Fax: 287 7183, Open D & Sun L, D€€, L€€)

RATHNEW
Tinakilly House Hotel is now in the hands of the second generation of the Power family, and it's a beautiful, grand dream of a house, perennially popular. (Rathnew, Tel: (0404) 69274, Fax: 67806, reservations@tinakilly.ie, tinakilly.ie, Open L&D, L€€, D€€€, Rates €€€)

ROUNDWOOD
The Roundwood Inn serves

good gutsy food which reveals the German background of the owners, lots of rich stews and goulashes. Above all, it is a reliable place, and a lovely stop –over if you are touring or walking in this area.
(Roundwood, Tel: (01) 281 8107, Open D & Sun L, D€€, L€€)

WICKLOW
The Bakery Restaurant Sally Steven's restaurant is one of the prettiest rooms you will find anywhere, and the cooking has a sure, feminine touch which is very pleasing indeed. Its pretty, comfortable decor means the Bakery is also a very good big date restaurant. (Church St, Wicklow, Tel: (0404) 66770, Fax: 66717, Open D, D€€)

ROUND UP THE USUAL SUSPECTS:
The Famous Sunday Lunch – or Linner, as they have named it – in the Hungry Monk often includes:

- Home-made Soup
- Warm Salad of Garlic Mushrooms
- Smoked Chicken breast and poached Pear salad
- Salad of Mozzarella, Beef Tomatoes, Pesto

- Roast Beef, Yorkshire Pudding, Fresh Horseradish Sauce
- Roulade of Lemon Sole stuffed with Crab and Spinach
- Limerick Ham with Parsley Sauce
- Spanakopita - Feta and Spinach Filo parcels

Belfast Central

● Michael Deane's eponymous restaurant, **Deane's**, has high prices, baroque décor, and some seriously imaginative cooking. Deane has carved out a singular style which uses bourgeois ingredients – he loves foie gras; loves scallops; loves game dishes – and then mixes these with fusion elements that reveal the pairings to be brilliantly logical. It's a brave chef who puts bak choi into a dish of monkfish with chorizo and Serrano ham, but when you taste Deane's version you wonder why everyone else doesn't do it. This sort of revelation, this exploration of food and its boundaries, makes for thrilling, distinctive cooking. Expensive, of course, but by and large well worth it. There is also a brasserie downstairs, but this has been woefully inconsistent in recent times. (38-40 Howard St, Belfast BT1 6PD, Tel: 903 31134, Fax: 905 60001, deanesbeflast.com, deanesbelfast@deanesbelfast.com, Open D, D€€€)

● Paula and Jeanne Rankin's flagship **Cayenne** restaurant is part of their Roscoff chain which includes the brilliant **Roscoff Café** and **Bakery** on Fountain Street (don't miss it) and the **Roscoff Café** and **Express** on Arthur Street (don't waste time on it). Cayenne is fabulous, original and fun, but a little too left-field and conceptual in style for some folk. The food can be uneven, but when on song this modern, multi-ethnic cooking from Paul Rankin and Andy Rea is nothing less than outstanding: orecchiette with chicken ragoût; char-grilled squid with chorizo and rocket; seafood risotto with Thai green curry; steamed salmon with lemon grass; and great desserts such as chocolate pound cake with honeycomb and baked citrus cheesecake. We don't like the two-sittings policy in the evening, however, and hope they change this. (1 Lesley House, Shaftesbury

Sq, Belfast BT2, Tel: 903 31532,
Fax: 903 12093, Open L & D, L€€, D€€.
Roscoff Cafe & Bakery, Fountain St, Tel:
903 5090, Open L, L€)

● Nick Price may be the
senior statesman of Belfast
eating, but he cooks like a
youngster, and his wit and
humour are undimmed by a
lifetime at the stove. His good humour is
explained, perhaps, by the fact that as he
gets older, he simply cooks better and
better. His wonderful **Nick's
Warehouse,** on High Street, takes its
lively cooking and ambience direct from
the joie de vivre of the boss and his wife,
Kathy, and it's a Don't Miss It! destination.
The food is comfort food with a cutting
edge, which might sound strange until
you eat it and see just how Price pulls it
off: soulful lamb shanks with red wine;
great local sausages and mash – this sort
of classic bistro fare done as well as you
will find anywhere - Moyallon pork with
rosemary, and the fish and vegetarian
cookery is excellent, as is the very
snappy, funny wine list which is an
entertainment even before they pull the
cork on a bottle for you. Part of the fabric
of the city, no less, and everyone needs
a baptism into Nick's. (35-39 Hill St,
Belfast, BT1 2LB, nickswarehouse.co.uk,
nicks@warehouse.dnet.co.uk, Open L&D,
L€, D€€)

NEW KID ON THE BLOCK

■ **Porcelaine**
Porcelaine is as
ambitious as it gets. A
smart restaurant, smart
rooms, a member's club,
and some searing fusion
food from chef Niall
McKenna add up to the
most ambitious opening
since Roscoff hit the
streets back in 1989.
The food has style and
execution: seared spicy
pork belly with Napa
slaw; fillet of beef with
Japanese horseradish
and parsley gratin; sea
bass with somen noodles
with an asparagus and
truffle dressing; seared
rare tuna with a
Szechwan pepper sauce;
rock shrimp tempura;
chocolate and raspberry
Christion; warm
chocolate and nut
samosas, with pistachio
ice cream. It's fusion, but
not fusion as Belfast has
ever seen before, and one
hopes there are enough
lovers of exotica to make
Porcelaine the hit it
deserves to be. Service is
keen, prices are good,
views are great.
(Ten Square, 10 Donegall
Sq Sth, Belfast BT1 5JD,
Tel: 9024 1001, Open L&
D, L€€, D€€€,
Accommodation €€€)

Northern Ireland – Belfast

● The other interesting destination in the centre city is the **Oxford Exchange Grill Bar,** beside the newly-smartened up St George's Market. A beautifully achieved architectural conversion, it also has good cooking: char-grilled sirloin with crispy onion rings and homemade chips; grilled sausages in a mixed grill; bistro specials such as onion soup with gruyere, and mussels with fennel and garlic; char-grilled chicken, and nursery puddings such as bread and butter pudding and crème anglaise. Good value, good service and good views. St George's Market, Tel: 9024 0014, Open daily, L€, D€.

SHOPPING & EATING

They take shopping seriously in Northern Ireland, and such serious activity demands decent food.

• There is some excellent pasta cookery to be found in Feasts, on the Dublin Road, where Craig Nash runs one of the best shops and cafés in the city. Most folk don't understand pasta, but Nash and his crew make sublimely simple pasta dishes with impeccable ingredients that can just blow you away. Great shop. (39 Dublin Rd, BT2, Tel: 9033 2787, Open L, L€)

• At the rere of the immensely stylish Equinox shop on Howard Street there is a swish little café where the coffees are particularly good (and are served in Rosenthal china). Cooking can be erratic, ambience is always delightful. (32 Howard St, Tel: 9023 0089, Open L€)

• Parks Café is a typically modern Belfast space, but the espresso is well made and their sweet things such as bakewell are good. Cool threads in the shop.

(Gt Victoria St. BT2, Tel: 9024 2394)

• Smyth & Gibson's Espresso Bar on Bedford Street has fine coffees, both to drink in or to go. Cool shirts out front. (Bedford House, Bedford St, BT2, Tel: 9023 0388, open daily)

• Fulton's models itself on Dublin's Avoca Handweavers, mixing cakes and bakes with an emporium space designed to liberate your cash with minimum pain. (Boucher Crescent, Tel: 9038 2168, Open L, L€)

Belfast food routes

⇨ LISBURN ROAD

● **Cargoes** is the locals' destination here, and
has been for many years now. Mary Maw and
Rhada Patterson are true food lovers: they not
only love to cook, they love to understand and
learn ever-more about food, its origins and its
cultures, the secrets and details that make
dishes work. And that deep culinary

background is evident here in the detail of the dishes, which are
always striving to be as definitive, and yet as improvised, as they can
possibly be: this is smashing cooking and a great place to eat, even if
you only have a sandwich and a cup of coffee.
(613 Lisburn Rd, BT9, Tel: 9066 5451, Open L, L€)

● The new boy on the Lisburn Road block is
Alan Reid's **Shu**, which has opened to
unanimous acclaim for Paul Catterson's
cooking. It's a slightly strange place:

cutting edge 21st century design with a
sushi bar, and yet classical brasserie cooking
which is actually just right for the setting:
omelette Arnold Bennett (yeah, we thought it had gone out with the
flood too); fish and chips with mushy peas (done posh, of course); a
signature dish of spiced chicken with chickpea casserole (always
good); good bread and butter pudding.
The tensions at work here actually conspire to create someplace
interesting and fun.
(253 Lisburn Rd, BT9, Tel: 9038 1655, Fax: 9038 1632,
shu-restaurant.com, eat@shu-restaurant.com, Open L & D, L€€, D€€)

Northern Ireland – Belfast

⇨ ORMEAU ROAD

● Simon McCance's brilliant **Ginger** restaurant has been the hottest hot shot in the city since opening last year, and this young chef and his team – and his low prices and BYO policy – mean that getting a table in Ginger is even more difficult than, for instance, following the story in that awesomely brilliant movie, Memento.

McCance cooks like a dream: assured, innovative, judged-just-right, with a true instinct for flavour: hake with spiced aubergine and garlic potatoes; scallops with crushed potato salad and basil; warm smoked salmon with roast tomatoes and lentils; roast plums with mascarpone. Great staff, and Ginger is as logical and delightful a place to eat as you will find. (217 Ormeau Rd, Tel: 9049 3143, Open D, D€€)

⇨ NEWTOWNARDS ROAD

Many food lovers will nominate Aldens, on the Upper Newtownards Road, as their absolute favourite Belfast restaurant, and Jonathan Davis' assured service, a truly lovely room, and knockout cooking from Cath Gradwell and her team makes for one of the great icon restaurants.

The food here is sublime, nothing less, and the combinations of ingredients and flavours can be pitch-perfect: sweetcorn and potato soup with red pepper jus; calves liver with mash, beurre noisette and capers; roast halibut with garlic mash and red wine sauce; braised shoulder of pork with lemon couscous and harissa; extraordinary desserts such as apple and plum bread and butter pudding; black pepper meringues with strawberries and vanilla cream; stewed gooseberries with custard. The energy is with this cooking and this room: don't miss it. (229 Upr Newtownards Rd, Belfast BT4 3JF, Tel: 906 50079, Fax: 9065 0032, Open L&D, L€€, D€€€)

● Just up the road, **The Olive Tree Company** is a darling little shop with a tiny café – seven tables – upstairs, which always has a great buzz at any time of day. Olivier Maindroult and his funky team understand their food and source it with care, so flavours are true and pleasing; curried aubergine soup; falafel in pitta with harissa; lovely simple desserts such as fresh fruit salad prepared with tender loving care. Great sounds, great crowd, and loads of vital foods to take home as you leave. A slice of genuine bohemia, and just what you need when you have turned 40. 353 Ormeau Rd, BT7, Tel: 9064 8898, olivier@olivetreeco.fsnet.co.uk, Open daily, L€.

Where to stay in Belfast:

■ **ASH ROWAN**
An extra-comfy B&B which wraps itself around you like a big old favourite blanket. Lovely breakfasts seem to last for most of the morning, and terrific hospitality from Sam and Evelyn Hazlett completes the picture.
(12 Windsor Av, Belfast BT9 6EE, Tel: 9066 1758, Fax: 9066 3227, ashrowan@hotmail.com, Rates €€)

■ **HALCYON HOUSE**
Mary Potter's pretty house is another fine B&B in the Belfast bourgeois belt.
(68 Wellington Park, Malone Rd, BT9, Tel: 9068 1648, Rates: €)

■ **THE McCAUSLAND HOTEL**
The McCausland has a fantastic location, a stone's throw from the Albert Clock in the centre of town, and the rooms are very fine indeed, though the restaurant downstairs has yet to find consistent form. (34-38 Victoria St, Belfast BT1 3GH, Tel: 9022 0200, Fax: 90220220, info@mccauslandhotel.co.uk, Rates €€€)

■ **THE CRESCENT TOWNHOUSE**
Part of the Metro and Bar Twelve complex, just off Botanic Ave. The rooms are comfortable and well considered, and it's a great location, in the University Zone. (13 Lwr Crescent, BT7, Tel: 9032 3349, Rates €€€)

Northern Ireland – Belfast

⇨ UNIVERSITY ZONE

● **Zego** is the new kid on the block here, at the bottom of Botanic Avenue, and whilst Aidan Rooney's smart place tries a little too hard to be all things to all men at all times, there is some serious culinary intelligence at work, which makes this a promising venture.

Good fresh pastas are done just right and the basic concept of Italian food – simple preparations using good ingredients – is well thought through: polenta coated deep-fried squid; pancetta tart with new potatoes; chicken with chorizo risotto; a good chocolate truffle cake.
(32 Botanic Avenue, Belfast, Tel: 9080 8088, Open L&D, L€, D€€)

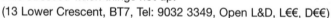

● There is some interesting cooking also in the **Metro Brasserie** just up and across the street from Zego, and whilst it's standard-modern it is well executed; duck with honey and soy butter; organic salmon with colcannon cake; rib-eye steak with chips and Creole mustard. Good value, and service is polite though can get a little stressed when things hot up.
(13 Lower Crescent, BT7, Tel: 9032 3349, Open L&D, L€€, D€€)

● **Beatrice Kennedy** on University Road is one of those places which deserves your custom for the simple reason that it follows no design or food fashions.
The interior is old style, the cooking is classical with little twists – duck bourguignonne; salmon with bacon dressing; spiced venison with caponata; sticky toffee pudding with butterscotch sauce.
(44 University Rd, BT7, Tel: 9020 2290, Open L&D, L€€, D€€)

Ethnic Belfast

● **The Water Margin** is one of the most exciting restaurants to open up in Belfast. Fronted and owned by charismatic Edmund Lau, formerly of the Sun Kee and part owned by Tony Cheuk of the Water Margin in Coleraine. Not as nice  inside as the beautiful stained glass windows suggest, but wow, what a place! Amazing dim sum served daily and scintillating, authentic Chinese food at night. Don't miss it. (Donegall Pass, Tel: 9032 6888, open L&D, L€, D€€)

● **The Sun Kee** remains possibly the ultimate cult restaurant in the entire country thanks to brilliant food – salt and chilli prawns are as good as it gets; crispy skinned duck with orange is brilliant; grilled aubergine with black bean and chilli is to die for; lettuce-wrapped pork with hoi sin is knockout. (38 Donegal Pass, Belfast BT7 1BS, Tel: 9031 2016, Open D, D€€)

● **The Manor House**, across the street from the Sun Kee, is a more traditional concept of a Chinese restaurant in Ireland and the food is good. (43-47 Donegall Pass, Belfast BT7 1DQ, Tel: 9023 8755, Open L&D, L€, D€€-€€€)

● **The Wok** on Gt Victoria St, offers pan-Asian food, which doesn't sound like a good idea, but which they do quite well: sugar-cane prawns; bang bang chicken. There isn't a lot of character in the room, but the food is reason to return. (126 Gt Victoria St, BT2, Tel: 9023 3828, Open L&D, €€)

● There is some interesting Thai food in the **Suwanna Thai Restaurant**, also on Great Victoria Street, but this place is so busy that it's almost impossible for the staff to cope. (Gt Victoria St, BT2, Tel: 9043 9007, Open D, €€)

GASTRO-PUBS

Belfast has been trying hard to catch up with the gastro-pub phenomenon, with interesting results.

● You will find good simple food in **The John Hewitt**, on Donegall Street in Belfast's Cathedral quarter – grilled trout with basil mayonnaise; smoked haddock with bubble and squeak, excellent crème brulée – and the fact that this is run by an unemployment resource center and is a not-for-profit venture makes the good food and good value even better.
(Donegall St, Tel: 9023 3768, Open L, L€)

● **TaTu**, at the top of the Lisburn Road, is a hot spot for design lovers (it's a beautiful piece of design and architecture) and the food is identikit-modern, but inconsistent so far: give them a bit more time.
(701 Lisburn Rd, Belfast BT9 7GU, Tel/Fax: 9038 0818, Open L&D, L€, D€€)

● There is bad design but good food in **The Edge** in the Lagan quarter, where chef Donal Keane does some lovely simple and powerful things such as Cullybackey asparagus with hollandaise and halibut with chive butter and great desserts such as burnt caramel ice cream. Service needs to be smartened up and the design simplified, however.
(Mays Meadow, Lagan Bank Rd, Belfast BT1, Tel: 9032 2000, Open L&D, L€€, D€€)

● **The Northern Whig** on Bridge Street is a big, tall, rather silly and very busy pub with some decent food: beef and stout sausages with champ; tuna loin with char-grilled vegetables; tempura monkfish.
(2 Bridge St, Belfast BT1, Tel: 9050 9888, Open daily L&early D, L€, D€€)

Antrim North Coast

● **The Ramore** restaurant in Portrush Harbour continues to undergo its periodic transformations, and now offers three separate dining areas. In **Coast,** you choose between pastas and pizzas, you can even make up your own pizza by choosing what ingredients you fancy. (Tel: 7082 3311, Open L&D, L€, D€)

● In **The Ramore Wine Bar** (formerly the restaurant) you choose from a large menu with three separate sections devoted to chicken, meat and fish dishes – char-siu chicken breast; trimmed sirloin with prawn croissants; Japanese tempura prawns. (Tel: 7082 4313, Open L&D, L€, D€)

● There is a similar but smaller menu in **The Harbour Bistro,** typically kebabs, steaks, roasts and such like. These are attractively decorated spaces, and the food is generally reliable and the buzz is good. (Tel: 7082 2430 Open from 4.30pm, D€€)

Where to stay:

• MADDYBENNY FARMHOUSE
Rosemary White's Maddybenny Farmhouse is a legendary B&B, with gargantuan, lengthy, fun breakfasts. (18 Maddybenny Park, Portrush, Tel: 7082 3394, Fax: 7082 3394, maddybenny.freeserve.co.uk. Rates ¤¤)

• THE MOAT INN
Robert and Rachel Thompson's house is that rarity in Northern Ireland, a true style-lover's destination. Lovely cooking only adds to the enchantment of a darling house. Don't miss it. (12 Donegore Hill, Templepatrick, BT41 2HW, Tel: 9443 3659, Fax: 9443 3726, themoatinn@talk21.com, Rates €€)

Down: north county

● **Shanks** is one of the few Gourmet Pilgrimage Destinations in Ireland, and food lovers make their way to just outside Bangor to pay homage to Robbie and Shirley Millar's outstanding restaurant.

Actually, the great thing is that no one pays homage, because the Millars don't stand on any ceremony, however much their skills might entitle them to. The restaurant is simple, the service impeccable, the cooking sublime: put the three together and you get true greatness.

Millar's signature dishes are amazing: gratin of lobster with coconut, curry and caramelized cauliflower; seared foie gras with potato bread and savoy cabbage; gingered tempura of monkfish with Chinese black bean sauce; tapenade crusted cod with black pasta; daube of beef with polenta mash; the incredible chocolate tart; carrot steamed pudding with cardamon custard. In every way, this is a benchmark restaurant. (The Blackwood, 150 Crawfordsburn Rd, Clandeboye, BT19 1GB, Tel: 9185 3313, Fax: 9185 2493, Open L&D, L€€€, D€€€)

Robbie's predictions:

Where Robbie Millar leads, others often follow, so we asked him: what are your new discoveries for the next season?

'I'm using porcini oil at the moment, and it's just gorgeous, a bit like truffle oil, but that real cep flavour. I use it with veal – I put it with a potato and Parmesan purée with wild mushrooms, and also with ravioli of foie gras with fresh corn and porcini oil. I'm looking forward to putting it on in the autumn with the porcini we have in the estate.

'I'm also enjoying using toasted marshmallow. It's one of those great childhood memories, with the meringue caramelised on the outside, soft in the middle. We make Italian meringue, whisk until cold, pipe little pillows of it, then blow torch. Some people have described it as shells on the beach, others snow peaks on a mountain. I serve it with fresh mango.'

● In Bangor, meantime, the smartest choice is a smart chipper: **The Bangor Fish Company** on High Street is now run by Philip Ash, a true devotee of great fish 'n' chips, and his devotion reveals how fried fish and chips can be raised to an art form: take a big bag of crisp chips and some lively battered fish down to the marina and sit on the wall (in the rain) and it's some sort of Bangor bliss, for sure.
(20 High St, Bangor, Tel: 9147 2172, Open daily, L€, D€)

● The locals around north Down all head to Donaghadee to the popular **Bistro Bistro**, a part of the legendary Grace Neill's pub (oldest pub in Ireland and all that) where Steven Jeffers manages to cook trencherman stuff for golfing sorts, whilst also indulging himself with some culinary excitements for food lovers: duck and shiitake terrine with baby leeks; clear crab soup with linguini and mussels; lemon risotto with langoustines; Banh trang pork parcels; sea bass with fennel and new potatoes, and some lovely puddings. Ambition sometimes outreaches the level of execution, but the value, the friendliness and the sheer energy of the food make Bistro Bistro a big big hit.
(33 High Street, Donaghadee, Tel: 9188 4595 graceneills.co.uk, Open L&D, L€, D€€)

● The other Donaghadee destination is Margaret and Denis Waterworth's friendly **Pier 36.**
The Waterworths are enthusiastic – hell, passionate – about their food and their business, and their bonhomie and youthfulness make this a great place. They barbecue their salmon on mesquite, layer crisp pancetta between French toast; make a brewy cassoulet with fine Moyallon wild boar; and make good Mom 'n' pop desserts along with the excellent bread baked on the Rayburn. Simple, really charming and loveable.
(36 The Parade, Donaghadee, Tel; 9188 4466 pier36.co.uk, Open L&D, L€, D€€)

Holywood: gourmet ghetto

Holywood may be dying on its feet, thanks to the malign influence of nearby hypermarkets, but the town is still a true gourmet ghetto, amongst which the star is Colleen Bennett's Fontana restaurant.

■ Ms Bennett is a fine cook, and above all an improving, inquisitive cook. The weak areas of her repertoire have been sorted out thanks to hard work, and **Fontana** now produces some of the most delicious cooking in the North: fennel and mushroom salad with beef bruschetta; char-grilled veal with gremolata; pork ribs with rice; skate wings with spinach and mash; frozen espresso crème brulée.
It's magpie cooking, pulling in ideas from all over the globe, but the sureness of execution is terrific and the value for money and the bright upstairs room are right on the money. When they tighten up the service, Fontana will have it all.
(61a High Street, Holywood Tel: 9080 9908 Open L&D, L€, D€€)

■ Everyone in Holywood loves Sue Farmer's cooking at **The Bay Tree**, and the cult local secret here is getting a table for dinner on Friday nights, the only time Ms Farmer cooks dinner. This is marvellously relaxed, confident, moreish food, and it's obviously a family affair: Ms Farmer is a sister of Nick Price of Nick's Warehouse in Belfast. This is mature cooking, and you never tire of goat's cheese salad with good leaves, walnuts and Puy lentils; spinach flan; haddock with parsley sauce; and great desserts: pecan and chocolate brownie; (the sweet baking is great). A vital place.
(118 High Street, Holywood Tel: 9042 1419 Open daily, L €)

■ Simon Shaw has made a great success of his re-styled **Sullivan's**, another hugely popular local place, where good cooking is the star. Mr Shaw's food is accessible and enjoyable, and his clientele of all ages reflects the style of a man who cooks to please.
(Sullivan Place Tel: 9042 1000 Open L & D, L€, D€€)

■ The best local ethnic choice (Holywood has a rake of ethnic take-aways) is **The Ganges**, where the décor is awful and the food is good: chicken tikka masala; king prawn dhansak; a large range of tandoori dishes and lots of vegetarian choices. The Ganges also does a big take-away trade
(47-49 High Street Tel: 9042 1218 L&D, €)

Down South County

● Alison and Michael Carruthers have created a great reputation with their cooking in **The Buck's Head Inn**, in Dundrum. Again, there is plenty of Ulster fare for conservative tastes, but the imagination evident in the more cutting-edge dishes is wholly admirable: scampi spring roll packed with ginger and al dente vegetables is beautifully done; excellent rack of lamb with Madeira and green peppercorn reduction; super light panna cotta. The use of lots of local foods is especially meritorious.
(77 Main St, Dundrum, BT33 OLU, Tel: 4375 1868, Fax: 4375 1898, Open L&D, L€, D€€)

● In Gilford, young Barry Smyth has made a great food lover's destination in **The Oriel**, a singularly unattractive building in the middle of nowhere in particular, where everyone in this neck of the woods heads to because the cooking is just so fine. Mr Smyth cooks really moreish, cherishable food: seared trout with tapenade and sauce gribiche; chilli beef with baby potato salad, horseradish and wasabi; mushroom-crusted venison; pearl barley with wild boar, and he is at his best giving exciting new slants to old classics such as roast beef. Excellent desserts are another signature of The Oriel. (Gilford, nr Banbridge, Tel: 3883 1543, Fax: 3883 1180, orielrestaurant@aol.com, Open L&D, L€€, D€€-€€€)

WARRENPOINT

The success story of south Down is Ciaran Gallagher's Duke's Restaurant, above Duke's Bar on Duke Street (boy, that's a lot of Dukes).

He packs them in during the week with a menu at £10.95. He serves classics such as surf 'n' turf, scampi and chicken Kiev for cautious folk, but he makes them properly, and then he also allows food lovers some serious dishes at the weekend when he cooks the glam stuff: grilled turbot with wilted bok choi and prawn bisque cream; Dover sole with garlic butter, fresh spinach and smoked bacon; tuna loin, with mango and spiced guacamole; lobster in brandy and cream; roast barramundi with lemon and basil risotto, and a sweet pea broth. This cook is serious, and Duke's is the destination way down south. (Warrenpoint, Tel: 4175 2084, Open D, D€)

Down

Down Ulster Way

● The key address in north Down is Victoria Brann's languid and pretty **Beech Hill Country House**, which sits proud on the hill on the Ballymoney Road, which is sort-of-in-between Holywood, Bangor, Craigantlet and Newtownards. Most importantly, it's not far from everywhere, but it feels miles from anywhere, and the cooking and housekeeping are exceptional.
(23 Ballymoney Rd, Craigantlet, Newtownards, Tel: 9042 5892, Fax: 9042 5892, beech-hill.net, beech.hill@btinternet.com, Rates €€)

● In south County Down, two pretty B&B's are the best choices. Maureen Thornton's **Strangford Cottage** is up on the hill in the middle of a terrace in pretty little Strangford and it's a dramatic, stylish house with a strong dash of theatricality, much like the owner herself; this is a memorable address, and a real style lover's hideaway.
(Strangford, BT30 7NF, Tel: 4488 1208, Fax: 4488 1246, Rates €€)

● Not too far away, Janis and Ian Bailey's **Pheasants Hill** is hard by the road running from Downpatrick to Killyleagh, and aside from the fact that the house is actually on The Ulster Way and therefore a great base for walking and exploring, it is a vital address because the Baileys have an in-conversion holding and on this they rear their own pigs, which means the sausages and bacon they serve for breakfast are truly sublime. The house is domestic and comfy, and the breakfasts are a true treat: don't miss them.
(37 Killyleagh Road, Downpatrick, Tel: 4461 7246, pheasantshill@dnet.co.uk Rates €€)

Derry: the knowledge

The hotshot in recent months in 'Derry has been way up on the north coast. **Smyths**, in The Diamond in Portstewart, has real cooking in a room with pleasing modern décor. Starters are unusual – savoury cheesecake; pate of wild mushrooms en croute, for instance – and whilst handsome and indeed painterly, they can incline to be a slightly heavy way to begin a meal. But the savoury cooking is spot on, and shows splendid judgement and appreciation of basic flavours: loin of lamb with mint, garlic and chilli with creamed leeks; magret of duck on a cinnamon and orange risotto; and it's charming that they even do a steak dinner, a sirloin served with fried onions, mushrooms, tomatoes and home-made chips! Steak garni lives on in Portstewart! At the present moment, Smyth's has no licence, so bring your own wine.
(2-4 Lever Rd, Portstewart, Tel: 7083 3564, Open D and weekend L£, D€€)

• Gardiner's restaurant in Magherafelt, in south County 'Derry, is a destination address in an area with few places to offer. (Garden St Tel: 7930 0333 Open L&D, L€, D€€)

• A hugely popular Chinese restaurant is Tony Cheuk's The Water Margin, in Coleraine, a place which is reassuringly patronized by other N.I. Chinese restaurateurs. It's a big buzzy room, and if you tell them you want the real thing then you will get it. (Tel: 7034 2222, Open D, €€)

• In Limavady, the destination address is Stanley and Maria Matthews' The Lime Tree, on Catherine St, which locals love for its friendly service from Mrs Matthews and for well-delivered popular food. (Tel: 7776 4300. Open L&D, L€, D€€)

• In 'Derry itself, The Leprechaun is a good lunchtime spot for homey food whilst Florentini's on Clooney Terrace is good for ice cream and decent chips.

index

C

The Bridgestone 100 Best Series

• THE BRIDGESTONE
100 BEST PLACES TO STAY IN IRELAND 2002

This is the most authoritative and up-to-the-minute guide to Ireland's finest hotels, country houses and bed and breakfasts.

'No-one who drives in Ireland, north or south, should travel without a copy in the glove box of their car.'

THE SUNDAY BUSINESS POST

• THE BRIDGESTONE
100 BEST RESTAURANTS IN IRELAND 2002

The Bridgestone 100 Best Restaurants in Ireland 2002 guides you to the most creative and cutting-edge restaurants throughout the country.

'When you read and use the guides, it is impossible not to be deeply impressed and to ask yourself whether, these days, Ireland might indeed have one of the finest food cultures in Europe.'

THE GUARDIAN

• HOW TO RUN A RESTAURANT

In this provocative book, John McKenna offers a radical analysis of how restaurants operate, and why some restaurants succeed where others fail.

Examining the business from the position of a customer and a critic, McKenna analyses the factors which contribute to success, and explores the decisions which have to be understood by anyone who is either already running a restaurant or considering opening a new restaurant.
Practitioners and students will find the book an exhilarating intellectual exploration of one of the most mercurial and fascinating industries and entertainments in the world.
'The McKennas are the most powerful food writing team in the country. They are exciting and talented critics.'
The Sunday Business Post

The Companion to this guide is...

The Bridgestone food lover's guides to Ireland:

The Shopper's Guide

● The Shopper's Guide is for the resident who wants to know the best places to find good food in their town, city or county. It is for the traveller who wants reliable and accurate information about the don't-miss-'em places to shop throughout Ireland. It is for the tourist who wants to discover the magic of Ireland's artisan food culture.

● With humour and insight, The Shopper's Guide describes the very best that Ireland has to offer, from what you need to know about your supermarket, to just how to track down that hard-to-find black pudding made by that lady somewhere in County Clare.

● The Shopper's Guide simply tells you who makes the best, and where to get your hands on it. It is not a factotum of Ireland's tourism industry, which feels obliged to list each and every place to shop. Instead, it is a highly critical, highly selective guide, which unveils to the shopper the very best that Ireland has to offer.

● And in discovering the very best that Ireland has to offer, you will discover one of the most exciting, inspiring food cultures in the world.

'You are paying quite a bit over the apparent value, partly for that discrimination that won't let you be given rubbish or ripped off, partly for some fun. We admire Estragon for this: produce an extra good product and charge a bit over the odds. Let other people do the pedestrian all-inclusive guides.'   **BOOKS IRELAND**

Up-to-the minute news and any relevant changes in the Bridgestone Guides can be found by visiting...

bridgestoneguides.com

VISIT...

bridgestoneguides.com

and sign up to Megabytes, the free newsletter of the Bridgestone Guides.

FEATURES INCLUDE

- Up-to-date information about the world of Irish food

- Regular campaigns to protect our food culture

- Monthly recipes

- A look at menus from both Ireland and abroad

- Features and recipes by some of Ireland's leading chefs

- Readers' letters

- Competitions with great foodie prizes

- A free noticeboard for the trade, buying and selling anything from a front-of-house to a side of organic pork!

LUS

The Megabytes Club!

Special Offers!

Irish food and wine ordered directly through the web.